D0601957

Psychological
Disorders

Attention-Deficit/
Hyperactivity Disorder

Psychological Disorders

Psychological Disorders

Attention-Deficit/ Hyperactivity Disorder

Jeremy Peirce, Ph.D.

Series Editor
Christine Collins, Ph.D.
Research Assistant Professor of Psychology
Vanderbilt University

Foreword by
Pat Levitt, Ph.D.
Director, Vanderbilt Kennedy Center
for Research on Human Development

CHELSEA HOUSE
P U B L I S H E R S
An imprint of Infobase Publishing

Psychological Disorders: Attention-Deficit/Hyperactivity Disorder

Chelsea House
An imprint of Infobase Publishing
132 West 31st Street
New York NY 10001

Library of Congress Cataloging-in-Publication Data
Peirce, Jeremy L., 1972-
  Attention-deficit/hyperactivity disorder / Jeremy Peirce ; consulting editor, Christine Collins ; foreword by Pat Levitt.
      p. ; cm. — (Psychological disorders)
  Includes bibliographical references and index.
  ISBN-13: 978-0-7910-8541-7 (hardcover : alk. paper)
  ISBN-10: 0-7910-8541-4 (hardcover : alk. paper) 1. Attention-deficit hyper-activity disorder. I. Collins, Christine E. (Christine Elaine) II. Title. III. Series: Psychological disorders (Chelsea House Publishers)
  [DNLM: 1. Attention Deficit Disorder with Hyperactivity. WS 350.8.A8 P378a 2008]
  RJ506.H9P45 2008
  616.85'89—dc22   2007035325

Text design by Keith Trego
Cover design by Keith Trego and Ben Peterson

Printed in the United States of America

Bang EJB 10 9 8 7 6 5 4 3 2 1

This book is printed on acid-free paper.

All links and Web addresses were checked and verified to be correct at the time of publication. Because of the dynamic nature of the Web, some addresses and links may have changed since publication and may no longer be valid.

Table of Contents

Foreword

Pat Levitt, Ph.D.
Vanderbilt Kennedy
Center for Research
on Human Development

Think of the most complicated aspect of our universe, and then multiply that by infinity! Even the most enthusiastic of mathematicians and physicists acknowledge that the brain is by far the most challenging entity to understand. By design, the human brain is made up of billions of cells called neurons, which use chemical neurotransmitters to communicate with each other through connections called synapses. Each brain cell has about 2,000 synapses. Connections between neurons are not formed in a random fashion, but rather are organized into a type of architecture that is far more complex than any of today's supercomputers. And, not only is the brain's connective architecture more complex than any computer; its connections are capable of *changing* to improve the way a circuit functions. For example, the way we learn new information involves changes in circuits that actually improve performance. Yet some change can also result in a disruption of connections, like changes that occur in disorders such as drug addiction, depression, schizophrenia, and epilepsy, or even changes that can increase a person's risk of suicide.

Genes and the environment are powerful forces in building the brain during development and ensuring normal brain functioning, but they can also be the root causes of psychological and neurological disorders when things go awry. The way in which brain architecture is built before birth and in childhood will determine how well the brain functions when we are adults, and even how susceptible we are to such diseases as depression, anxiety, or attention disorders, which can severely disturb brain function. In a sense, then, understanding how the brain is built can lead us to a clearer picture of the ways in which our brain works, how we can improve its functioning, and what we can do to repair it when diseases strike.

Brain architecture reflects the highly specialized jobs that are performed by human beings, such as seeing, hearing, feeling, smelling, and moving. Different brain areas are specialized to control specific functions. Each specialized area must communicate well with other areas for the brain to accomplish even more complex tasks, like controlling body physiology—our patterns of sleep, for example, or even our eating habits, both of which can become disrupted if brain development or function is disturbed in some way. The brain controls our feelings, fears, and emotions; our ability to learn and store new information; and how well we recall old information. The brain does all this, and more, by building, during development, the circuits that control these functions, much like a hard-wired computer. Even small abnormalities that occur during early brain development through gene mutations, viral infection, or fetal exposure to alcohol can increase the risk of developing a wide range of psychological disorders later in life.

Those who study the relationship between brain architecture and function, and the diseases that affect this bond, are neuroscientists. Those who study and treat the disorders that are caused by changes in brain architecture and chemistry are psychiatrists and psychologists. Over the last 50 years, we have learned quite a lot about how brain architecture and chemistry work and how genetics contributes to brain structure and function. Genes are very important in controlling the initial phases of building the brain. In fact, almost every gene in the human genome is needed to build the brain. This process of brain development actually starts prior to birth, with almost all the neurons we will ever have in our brain produced by mid-gestation. The assembly of the architecture, in the form of intricate circuits, begins by this time, and by birth we have the basic organization laid out. But the work is not yet complete because billions of connections form over a remarkably long period of time, extending through puberty. The brain of a child is being built and modified on a daily basis, even during sleep.

While there are thousands of chemical building blocks, such as proteins, lipids, and carbohydrates, that are used much like bricks and mortar to put the architecture together, the highly detailed connectivity that emerges during childhood depends greatly upon experiences and our environment. In building a house, we use specific blueprints to assemble the basic structures, like a foundation, walls, floors, and ceilings. The brain is assembled similarly. Plumbing and electricity, like the basic circuitry of the brain, are put in place early in the building process. But for all of this early work, there is another very important phase of development, which is termed experience-dependent development. During the first three years of life, our brains actually form far more connections than we will ever need, almost 40 percent more! Why would this occur? Well, in fact, the early circuits form in this way so that we can use experience to mold our brain architecture to best suit the functions that we are likely to need for the rest of our lives

Experience is not just important for the circuits that control our senses. A young child who experiences toxic stress, like physical abuse, will have his or her brain architecture changed in regions that will result in poorer control of emotions and feelings as an adult. Experience is powerful. When we repeatedly practice on the piano or shoot a basketball hundreds of times daily, we are using experience to model our brain connections to function at their finest. Some will achieve better results than others, perhaps because the initial phases of circuit-building provided a better base, just like the architecture of houses may differ in terms of their functionality. We are working to understand the brain structure and function that result from the powerful combination of genes building the initial architecture and a child's experience adding the all-important detailed touches. We also know that, like an old home, the architecture can break down. The aging process can be particularly hard on the ability of brain circuits to function at their best because positive change comes less readily as we get older. Synapses may be lost and brain chemistry can change over time. The difficulties in understanding how architecture gets built are paralleled by the complexities of what happens to that architecture as we grow older. Dementia associated with brain deterioration as a complication of Alzheimer's disease and memory loss associated with aging or alcoholism are active avenues of research in the neuroscience community.

There is truth, both for development and in aging, in the old adage "use it or lose it." Neuroscientists are pursuing the idea that brain architecture and chemistry can be modified well beyond childhood. If we understand the mechanisms that make it easy for a young, healthy brain to learn or repair itself following an accident, perhaps we can use those same tools to optimize the functioning of aging brains. We already know many ways in which we can improve the functioning of the aging or injured brain. For example, for an individual who has suffered a stroke that has caused structural damage to brain architecture, physical exercise can be quite powerful in helping to reorganize circuits so that they function better, even in an elderly individual. And you know that when you exercise and sleep regularly, you just feel better. Your brain chemistry and architecture are functioning at their best. Another example of ways we can improve nervous system function are the drugs that are used to treat mental illnesses. These drugs are designed to change brain chemistry so that the neurotransmitters used for communication between brain cells can function more normally. These same types of drugs, however, when taken in excess or abused, can actually damage brain chemistry and change brain architecture so that it functions more poorly.

As you read the Psychological Disorders series, the images of altered brain organization and chemistry will come to mind in thinking about complex diseases such as schizophrenia or drug addiction. There is nothing more fascinating and important to understand for the well-being of humans. But also keep in mind that as neuroscientists, we are on a mission to comprehend human nature, the way we perceive the world, how we recognize color, why we smile when thinking about the Thanksgiving turkey, the emotion of experiencing our first kiss, or how we can remember the winner of the 1953 World Series. If you are interested in people, and the world in which we live, you are a neuroscientist, too.

Pat Levitt, Ph.D.
Director, Vanderbilt Kennedy Center
for Research on Human Development
Vanderbilt University
Nashville, Tennessee

Introduction

Sam Barnes and his sister Sarah were very different children. Sam was very active and always zipping between activities and games. When Sam went to preschool, he was quite a "handful" for the staff, often climbing furniture, running in the hallway, talking in the classroom, and not following instructions without reminders. At home, Sam frequently left his chores unfinished. Because a lot of pre-school children exhibit these behaviors to some degree, Sam's parents and teachers assumed his actions were the result of normal childhood "high spirits." Kindergarten and first grade brought no change, and in second grade Sam's behaviors started to affect his performance in school. By then other children who had behaved rambunctiously in kindergarten and first grade had become more restrained as they matured. Sam still had trouble sitting quietly during class and blurted out answers and sometimes unrelated questions at odd moments. He got up from his seat during lessons and sometimes refused to wait his turn during games and exercises. At home, Sam's relationship with his parents was worsening. Sam seemed to stop trying to do things his parents asked him to do, like clean his room or do his chores.

Homework was also a big challenge. Even when Sam remembered his books, he rarely finished his assignments. Sometimes he found the material frustrating, and other times he just couldn't sit still without one of his parents standing over him to keep him focused on his work. By January, Sam's grades were mostly failing, and he was close to being held back. Fortunately, he didn't have to repeat the grade. Sam was diagnosed with attention-deficit/hyperactivity disorder (ADHD). A patient teacher, the right medication, and frequent tutoring sessions tailored to Sam's learning patterns helped him earn passing grades.

Sarah, a year older than her brother Sam, displayed a very different pattern of behavior. A quiet child and more reserved than her younger brother, Sarah was more often described as "off in her own little world" or "absent minded," and her inability to follow through on instructions frustrated her parents and teachers.

About midway through the fourth grade, a year after Sam's diagnosis of ADHD in the second grade, Sarah's grades started slipping severely and her "spaciness" worsened. Sarah's teacher suggested to Mrs. Barnes that Sarah might also have ADHD. Mrs. Barnes and her husband had trouble believing it. After all, Sarah wasn't at all hyperactive. If anything she was sluggish and slow to respond. Her lack of attention to details and instructions seemed more due to daydreaming than an excess of nervous energy. Working with Sam was like swimming upstream against a constant flood of conversation that was often way off topic. Working with Sarah involved frequent pauses, and it was often hard to tell whether she was working out an answer or had "spaced" on the topic at hand. Despite these differences, both Sam and Sarah were correctly diagnosed, a little more than a year apart, with ADHD.

Attention-deficit/hyperactivity disorder is the name of a group of attention-related **symptoms** that are often found together, especially in children and young adults. The term is defined in a reference book the American Psychiatric Association (APA) publishes to help **psychiatrists** diagnose mental disorders, the

Diagnostic and Statistical Manual of Mental Disorders, usually called the **DSM** for short. There have been four main editions of this important handbook, and the most recent is often referred to as the *DSM-IV*. The *DSM-IV* gives definitions of many disorders and describes the expected symptoms for each. For ADHD, it lists three subtypes: Primarily **hyperactive** (like Sam), primarily **inattentive** (like Sarah), and combined. Often there are elements of each of the first two types in a particular person, and when there are enough, the **diagnosis** is ADHD–combined type.

If one sibling has ADHD, it is common for the other to have it as well, and among identical twins it is even more common. Much of the time, siblings even have the same subtype of ADHD, so Sam and Sarah are somewhat unusual in having different subtypes. Among identical twins with ADHD, this is particularly noticeable. When one twin has ADHD, the other also has it between 60 percent and 90 percent of the time. When both twins have ADHD, however, it is much more likely that they will have the same subtype.

Sam and Sarah are somewhat more typical in another way, however. It is about threefold more likely for boys to have primarily hyperactive ADHD symptoms, while girls much more often have primarily inattentive ADHD. Girls, however, can definitely have primarily hyperactive ADHD and boys can definitely have primarily inattentive ADHD. It's important for people diagnosing a child's ADHD to recognize this possibility, since the assumption that boys are affected only by primarily hyperactive ADHD and vice versa means that it often takes children with the type of ADHD less common for their gender longer to be correctly diagnosed and to receive correct treatment.

ADHD IN CONTEXT

A major difficulty in diagnosing ADHD is that almost every child is hyperactive and inattentive at times. Children must develop the ability to focus on tasks that are not very stimu-lating, are repetitive, or require a great deal of attention, like math problem sets or textbook reading assignments. Children with and without ADHD develop this ability over time, but for children with ADHD it takes longer and is more limited and difficult. Attention-deficit/hyperactivity disorder often becomes apparent in the middle elementary school years because of changing expectations. Between second and fifth grades, for instance, study material becomes more complex. This means that teachers require students to pay attention for longer peri-ods of time. This is also true at home, where parents and others give children more complex responsibilities.

People used to believe that ADHD was mostly a childhood and adolescent disorder. This is partly because people with ADHD often eventually learn to cope with some symptoms of the disorder, even if the symptoms don't disappear. Recently, however, researchers have learned that ADHD symptoms often continue into adulthood. At least a third of children diagnosed with ADHD will continue to have symptoms as adults and could benefit greatly from the same medications and approach-es used to treat children. In fact, since ADHD tends to cluster in families, adult ADHD is sometimes diagnosed in parents when a child is referred for ADHD treatment.

A BRIEF HISTORY OF ADHD ALPHABET SOUP: MBI, MBD, ADD, AND ADHD

Many other names have been used to describe more or less the same group of symptoms now called ADHD. In 1987, the official name the *DSM* gave to this disorder changed from attention deficit disorder, or ADD, to ADHD. ADD had a hyperactive subtype in this earlier version, (called ADD-H) but the writers of *DSM-IV* thought hyperactivity was an important enough facet of the disorder to add to the name, though hyperactivity is not required for a diagnosis of inattentive type ADHD.

This confusion is fairly widespread, and a number of the popular sources referenced in this book, such as Web sites, mix the terms ADHD and ADD, often but not always using ADD to refer to the primarily inattentive type of ADHD. In addition, some researchers have found evidence for as many as six subtypes of ADHD. The human brain is a complex organ, and the trend in research is to break down complex groups of symptoms like ADHD into more specific groupings. Given the differences between the subtypes of ADHD, it will not be surprising if more changes in the name are in store for the future.

Of course, when something has been around for a long time it tends to develop a number of names as people's perception of it changes. The group of symptoms now known as ADHD was described long before it was called ADD. Recognition of the disorder can be traced to the nineteenth century and psychologist William James' description of children with "explosive will" (1890) or to German physician and author Heinrich Hoffman's poem "The Story of Fidgety Philip" (1847), both of which describe hyperactive children. In 1902, George Still, an English pediatrician, presented to the Royal Society of Medicine cases from his clinical practice of children who had what he described as a "defect of moral control" and "volitional inhibition" that he believed might have a biological basis, as opposed to being a purely social or ethical failing (despite the term *moral*).

Dr. Still told the Royal Society about children who, despite good parenting, had problems with their behavior from an early age, including a lack of respect, defiance of authority, difficulty curbing bad behaviors even when disciplined, and serious problems with sustaining attention. He also noted that close relatives shared these characteristics and problems with alcoholism and the law more often than the average person

Figure 1.1 In 1902, English pediatrician George Still presented to the Royal Society of Medicine cases from his clinical practice of children who had what he described as a "defect of moral control" and "volitional inhibition" that he believed might have a biological basis. *U.S. National Library of Medicine, National Institutes of Health*

and that more male children had this group of symptoms. He even guessed that the disorder might sometimes be related to early traumas to the brain.

Twenty years later, researchers in the United States noticed similar symptoms in children who had suffered from encephalitis, a swelling of the brain caused by infection. The epidemic of encephalitis in 1917–1918 led to a large number of these children, who had survived the infection without apparent ill effect but who frequently suffered from attention and behavior problems.

The observation of ADHD symptoms in children exposed to encephalitis and in other cases with a known history of brain trauma led in the 1940s to Alfred Strauss and his collaborators suggesting the idea of minimal brain injury (MBI) as the cause for ADHD. Later, the similar term *minimal brain dysfunction* (MBD) evolved as similar symptoms were observed in children with no apparent history of brain trauma.

The idea that there was a biological basis for ADHD-like behaviors caught on very early—in North America, at least—much earlier than the idea of a biological basis for other disorders often thought of as having a moral component like alcoholism and other addictions. Another early contribution to the recognition of ADHD as a disorder with a largely physical basis was the discovery in 1937 by Dr. Charles Bradley that children with ADHD responded well to treatment with Benzedrine, a kind of **stimulant** medication called an **amphetamine**. Bradley noticed that Benzedrine, a common inhaled decongestant and asthma medicine, had a calming effect on his patients, who suffered from what he described as "organic behavior syndrome." For a few hours after taking Benzedrine, they were able to focus more effectively and were less impulsive.

Over the following three decades (1940–1970) doctors observed ADHD-like symptoms in many people with no

Fidgety Philip and Johnny Look-in-Air

Heinrich Hoffman (1809–1894), a German physician and author, wrote a number of poems about different types of children's foibles and the dreadful things that happen to them, both for entertainment and moral warning. Two of these poems seem to describe predominantly hyperactive/impulsive and primarily inattentive ADHD. These children's classics are still widely read today in the original German and in the English translations by Mark Twain.

The Story of Fidgety Philip

"Let me see if Philip can
Be a little gentleman;
Let me see if he is able
To sit still for once at table."
Thus spoke, in earnest tone,
The father to his son;
And the mother looked very grave
To see Philip so misbehave.
But Philip he did not mind
His father who was so kind.
He wriggled
And giggled,
And then, I declare,
Swung backward and forward
And tilted his chair,
Just like any rocking horse;
"Philip! I am getting cross!"

See the naughty, restless child,
Growing still more rude and wild,
Till his chair falls over quite.

Philip screams with all his might,
Catches at the cloth, but then
That makes matters worse again.
Down upon the ground they fall,
Glasses, bread, knives, forks and all.
How Mamma did fret and frown,
When she saw them tumbling down!
And Papa made such a face!
Philip is in sad disgrace.

Where is Philip? Where is he?
Fairly cover'd up, you see!
Cloth and all are lying on him;
He has pull'd down all upon him!
What a terrible to-do!
Dishes, glasses, snapt in two!
Here a knife, and there fork!
Philip, this is naughty work.
Table all so bare, and ah!
Poor Papa and poor Mamma
Look quite cross, and wonder how
They shall make their dinner now.

The Story of Johnny Look-in-the-Air
As he trudg'd along to school,
It was always Johnny's rule
To be looking at the sky
And the clouds that floated by;
But what just before him lay,
In his way,
Johnny never thought about;
So that every one cried out

(continues)

(continued)

"Look at little Johnny there,
Little Johnny Head-In-Air!"

Running just in Johnny's way,
Came a little dog one day;
Johnny's eyes were still astray
Up on high,
In the sky;
And he never heard them cry—
"Johnny, mind, the dog is nigh!"
What happens now?
Bump!
Dump!
Down they fell, with such a thump,
Dog and Johnny in a lump!
They almost broke their bones
So hard they tumbled on the stones.

Once, with head as high as ever,
Johnny walked beside the river.
Johnny watch'd the swallows trying
Which was cleverest at flying.
Oh! what fun!
Johnny watch'd the bright round sun
Going in and coming out;
This was all he thought about.
So he strode on, only think!
To the river's very brink,
Where the bank was high and steep,
And the water very deep;

And the fishes, in a row,
Stared to see him coming so.

One step more! Oh! sad to tell!
Headlong in poor Johnny fell.

The three little fishes, in dismay,
Wagged their tails and swam away.

There lay Johnny on his face;
With his nice red writing-case;
But, as they were passing by,
Two strong men had heard him cry;
And, with sticks, these two strong men
Hook'd poor Johnny out again.

Oh! you should have seen him shiver
When they pull'd him from the river
He was in a sorry plight,
Dripping wet, and such a fright!
Wet all over, everywhere,
Clothes, and arms, and face, and hair
Johnny never will forget
What it is to be so wet.

And the fishes, one, two, three,
Are come back again, you see;
Up they came the moment after,
To enjoy the fun and laughter.
Each popp'd out his little head,
And, to tease poor Johnny, said,
"Silly little Johnny, look,
You have lost your writing-book!"
Look at them laughing and do you see?
His satchel is drifting, far out to sea!

Figure 1.2 In 1937, Dr. Charles Bradley discovered that children with ADHD responded well to treatment with a type of amphetamine called Benzedrine. *U.S. National Library of Medicine, National Institutes of Health*

history or evidence of brain trauma, and the label of minimal brain dysfunction was replaced by more developmental labels such as "hyperactive child syndrome," "hyperkinesis" (abnormally high motion and muscular movement, sometimes uncontrollable), and, in the second edition of the *DSM*, "hyperkinetic reaction of childhood." These labels emphasized the ideas of hyperactivity, impulsivity, and lack of attention in the disorder. The change to the term attention deficit disorder and eventually to attention-deficit/hyperactivity disorder was part of this shift in understanding.

Today, while some differences have been observed between the brains of individuals with and without ADHD, they are not definite enough to diagnose the presence or absence of ADHD. The disorder clearly has a biological basis, but the vast majority of cases show no evidence of brain injury. There is strong evidence of **heritability**—the presence of the disorder in brothers, sisters, and near relatives—that, even when family environment is taken into consideration, indicates that a disorder has a genetic component.

THE ADHD EPIDEMIC

Current estimates of the percentage of children with ADHD in the United States vary between 3.5 percent and 7 percent, and the ratio of boys to girls with ADHD is usually about 3 to 1. While it is difficult to estimate how many ADHD diagnoses were made 10 to 15 years ago, the number was certainly much lower. This change has caused many people to speculate in recent years about the "ADHD epidemic" and whether it represents recognition of a real disorder that was previously under-diagnosed or a byproduct of parents and doctors overly concerned with their child's normal, highly active behavior.

One source of confusion in understanding the changing numbers of diagnosed cases of ADHD is that many mental disorders imitate aspects of ADHD, and some may be misdiagnosed as ADHD. A few of the more common disorders with overlapping symptoms are depression, learning disabilities, and oppositional defiant disorder. Finding out that a child

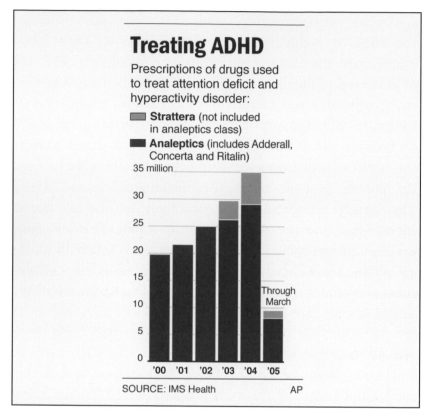

Treating ADHD

Prescriptions of drugs used
to treat attention deficit and
hyperactivity disorder:

▢ **Strattera** (not included
in analeptics class)
▉ **Analeptics** (includes Adderall,
Concerta and Ritalin)

SOURCE: IMS Health   AP

Figure 1.3 This graph illustrates the steady increase in prescriptions of drugs used to treat ADHD from 2000 to 2005. © *AP Images*

diagnosed with ADHD is depressed or suffers from another disorder, however, does not mean the ADHD diagnosis was wrong. Attention-deficit/hyperactivity disorder often coexists with the very disorders that imitate it.

A higher number of diagnoses can mean many things. The first possibility is that the disorder is **overdiagnosed**, meaning doctors make more diagnoses than there are people with genuine ADHD symptoms. Overdiagnosis can occur when the criteria for diagnosing a disorder change, when the disease is "popular" and often in the public eye, and when patients come to doctors with a specific disorder already in mind. The last happened to Jennifer, a very smart student with difficulty consolidating memory, or moving concepts and facts from her short-term memory to her long-term memory. For example, people will remember a new phone number easily for a few minutes but probably not the next day. On the other hand, they will easily remember their own phone number, because it has been consolidated into long-term memory. Jennifer's parents took her to several doctors before she was diagnosed with ADHD. They were convinced that she had that specific disorder and rejected the several doctors' opinions that Jennifer's difficulties were with memory rather than attention. They insisted that she try medication, which improved her focus a little—it has similar effects on people with and without ADHD—but really didn't help very much. Eventually, Jennifer received a more complete evaluation with help from her school district, and by focusing on ways to get around her poor memory, she improved her schoolwork quite a bit. Had Jennifer's parents been open minded about their daughter's problem, Jennifer might have gotten a correct diagnosis and help much sooner.

The second possibility is that a disorder is actually becoming more frequent in the population. Environmental reasons might cause this. For instance, one hypothesis might be that expanding demands on attention through cell phones, the Internet, socializing, television, and so on cause ADHD to be more apparent in modern settings than it was 15 years ago. Since ADHD also has a strong genetic component, a technical possibility is that the **alleles** (forms of a gene) underlying ADHD are becoming more common in the population. This is unlikely, though, because changes in alleles usually require thousands of years to occur.

The third possibility is that doctors are getting better at identifying ADHD. This is the same thing as saying that in the past people had the symptoms of ADHD but were not correctly diagnosed, so the disorder would have been **under-diagnosed**. Underdiagnosis can be the result of many possible causes, often the flip side of the causes of overdiagnosis. For instance, while overdiagnosis can result from the criteria for a diagnosis becoming less strict, underdiagnosis can result from the criteria for a diagnosis becoming stricter. Likewise, over-diagnosis may result from a disease becoming "popular" and underdiagnosis can result from a disease having a social stigma or being relatively unknown and thus "unpopular." It can be remedied by better education of doctors, more informative

ADHD Dividend: Creative Distraction

The symptoms of ADHD can negatively impact the lives of people who have the disorder, but the terms *symptoms* and *disorder* leave out the idea that having ADHD can also have remarkable benefits.

Many people with ADHD are very creative. From Thomas Edison's daydreams to Mozart's incredible bursts of creative genius, creativity has historically been associated with people whose attention differs from the norm. Many of the case histories given in this book are of people with remarkable creative focus—talented musicians, writers, designers, and programmers.

This is not to say that all creative people have ADHD, that all people who have ADHD are creative, or even that ADHD causes creativity, but clinicians and people with ADHD them-selves have remarked on the overlap. One interesting possibility is that there are underlying traits in common between highly creative people and people with ADHD, such as sensation and thrill seeking, intensity of concentration on interesting tasks, tests or guidelines for diagnosis, and better available treatments, which make it more useful to correctly diagnose the disorder. Another way to improve underdiagnosis is to provide access to resources that can help children and parents identify the effects of ADHD, such as psychiatrists, school psychologists, social workers, and educational specialists.

Treatment of ADHD with medication has also changed over time as the number of diagnoses has changed and as new medications and nonmedication approaches to treatment have become available. One important question is whether

and frequent daydreaming. These traits may be expressed in a particular person as increased creativity, ADHD, or both.

The idea that people with ADHD are more creative is not without controversy. Dione Healey and Julia Rucklidge at the University of Canterbury in New Zealand published an article in 2005 comparing the performance of children with and without ADHD on several tests of creative thinking and found that the two groups performed similarly. Another study by researchers at the Medical College of Ohio in 1993 found only a very small (7 percent) increase in nonverbal creativity associated with ADHD.

Even if the studies above are correct and people with ADHD are not innately more creative, it is certainly possible that people with ADHD are more drawn to creative jobs and outlets. These kinds of environments may tolerate and even reward behaviors that might be punished in situations with more rigidly defined right and wrong actions.

people with a diagnosis of ADHD are receiving appropriate medication. More use of medication than expected would indicate that ADHD is **overmedicated** and less medication than needed would indicate that ADHD is **undermedicated.** A 2005 study of information from more than 10,000 children ages 4–17, taken as part of the National Health Interview Survey, estimates the frequency of significant ADHD symptoms at 4.2 percent for males and 1.8 percent for females in the general population. However, 6.8 percent of males and 2.5 percent of females have a diagnosis of ADHD at some time in their lives but no symptoms (not all of these are necessarily misdiagnoses—some may also be individuals with mild symptoms that got better with age), and 1.6 percent of males and 0.8 percent of females had symptoms but no diagnosis. From these numbers, they concluded that overdiagnosis and underdiagnosis (as well as overmedication and undermedication) of ADHD occurs in the United States. There are people with a diagnosis and no symptoms as well as people with symptoms and no diagnosis.[1]

LEARNING ABOUT ADHD

ADHD is a complex, fascinating, and common mental disorder, highly studied as well as mysterious. The exact causes of ADHD are still being studied and are still largely unknown, though there are effective medications available to treat the disorder. Attention-deficit/hyperactivity disorder presents itself in many different ways, and the three subtypes recognized today—predominantly inattentive type, predominantly hyperactive-impulsive type, and combined type—could eventually expand to six or more. The disorder is heritable, which means its causes are often at least partly genetic, though there may be many genes and environmental influences involved. This book is a good place to start to explore the many things that are known about ADHD and to become familiar with some of the current controversies in the field. The one constant in science is that everything changes. The latest information about ADHD can be found on reliable Web sites and in other books and medical literature. There are lists of such sites and sources at the back of this book.

2 Different Types of ADHD

Since ADHD is defined by its symptoms rather than its cause, it is possible that the symptoms of the disorder could have one or many causes. The subtypes of ADHD could represent one disorder with symptoms that come out in different ways, or they could represent several different disorders with common symptoms. It is even possible, depending on the genetic components of the disorder(s), that both could be true, because ADHD is a genetically **heterogeneous** disease. This means that different genes may contribute to the group of symptoms called ADHD in different people, as opposed to there being one common group of genes behind the disease. This heterogeneity makes ADHD difficult to fully understand, but there is another layer of complexity to confront in diagnosing ADHD. Many other disorders and conditions can be mistaken for ADHD, as can many environmental conditions. When an environmental condition mimics ADHD, it is known as **phenocopy.** When studying ADHD, then, the first and most important question is, "Is this really ADHD?" An important follow-up question is, "Is this ADHD with a comorbidity?" Comorbidity refers to the presence of a disorder or disease with another disorder or disease. It can be difficult to distinguish between these possibilities, but information about people's symptoms can be organized into groups, and changes in these symptoms can be studied over time. The *Diagnostic and Statistical Manual of Mental Disorders* identifies three subtypes of behavior indicating ADHD: primarily hyperactive-impulsive type, primarily inattentive type, and combined type (which displays symptoms both hyperactive-impulsive and inattentive). Studies have shown that the combined ADHD subtype is the most persistent form of the disorder over time and the diagnosis that changes least over time.[2] The combined ADHD subtype is also the one most commonly used to investigate differences in drug effectiveness and other aspects of ADHD, because of its stability and because it is the most severe kind of ADHD.

THE PROGRESSION OF PRIMARILY HYPERACTIVE ADHD

In contrast to combined type ADHD, primarily hyperactive ADHD is often not a stable diagnosis. It is usually diagnosed early in childhood and either goes away with increasing age or becomes an ADHD combined type over time.[3]

Because primarily hyperactive ADHD seems to be more common in early childhood and tends to progress to combined type ADHD when it persists into the teen and adult years, one way to view it is to split the diagnosis into two groups. The first group includes people who have hyperactivity with no attention-related problems. The second group has hyperactivity and problems with attention, but the attention problems are not severe enough to qualify for a diagnosis of combined type ADHD. As children age and more demands are placed on their attention, especially in school, problems with attention become more apparent. For those in the first group, not much changes. For those in the second group, though, the diagnosis can shift to combined type ADHD as the attention portion of their disorder becomes more obvious.

PRIMARILY INATTENTIVE ADHD: BOREDOM OR DISTRACTION?

Primarily inattentive ADHD might also consist of two similar groups, one with severe difficulties in attention and one with

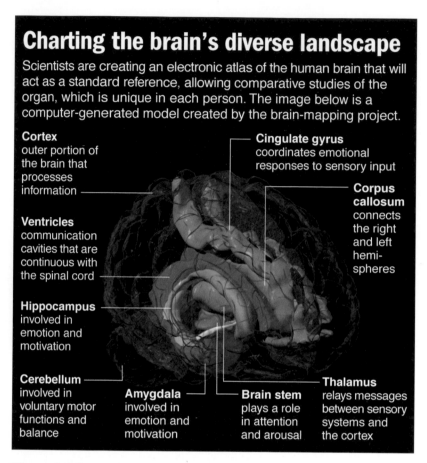

Charting the brain's diverse landscape

Scientists are creating an electronic atlas of the human brain that will act as a standard reference, allowing comparative studies of the organ, which is unique in each person. The image below is a computer-generated model created by the brain-mapping project.

Cortex
outer portion of the brain that processes information

Ventricles
communication cavities that are continuous with the spinal cord

Hippocampus
involved in emotion and motivation

Cerebellum
involved in voluntary motor functions and balance

Amygdala
involved in emotion and motivation

Cingulate gyrus
coordinates emotional responses to sensory input

Corpus callosum
connects the right and left hemi- spheres

Brain stem
plays a role in attention and arousal

Thalamus
relays messages between sensory systems and the cortex

Figure 2.1 Some researchers believe that primarily inattentive ADHD, without hyperactivity, is a separate disorder from primarily hyperactive ADHD, involving separate regions of the brain.
© *AP Images*

inattention plus hyperactivity too mild to be diagnosed as combined ADHD. Some researchers believe that severe inattentive ADHD, without hyperactivity, is a separate disorder involving separate regions of the brain.[4] Their idea is that a deficit in **working memory** is the basic problem behind inattentive "ADHD," not attention or inhibition of behavior as it is in combined and hyperactive type ADHD. Working memory is the kind of memory responsible for temporarily storing information, such as remembering a new phone number long enough to dial it. Working memory also involves processing—for instance, remembering part of the number while recalling the area code and putting it all together for dialing. The phone number is likely to be forgotten an hour later, but working memory keeps it "in mind" long enough for someone to add the area code, cross the room, and dial it.

A deficit in working memory would affect the selective part of attention—selecting a particular item to remember and manipulating it in one's mind. This would create problems in the working memory portion of **executive function**. Executive function is the overall ability to control and execute plans and intentions. The plan to make a phone call, for instance, might involve deciding to make the call, using working memory to keep that intention and a phone number in mind, and inhibiting attention to the TV long enough to actually accomplish the call. Difficulty holding things in mind could cause stronger, faster occurring boredom in someone with inattentive ADHD. This concept of ADHD distinguishes between boredom and distraction. People with inattentive ADHD might have difficulty paying attention because they are easily bored while people with combined type ADHD and possibly hyperactive type ADHD are easily distracted by outside influences and have difficulty with the third part of executive function, inhibiting attention to distracting influences. It is not yet clearly known whether all subtypes of ADHD are expressions of the same disorder or of different disorders.

ADHD TYPES AND COMORBIDITIES
One of the things that make ADHD difficult to understand and diagnose is that it is often **comorbid** with other disorders. Comorbidity can indicate a relationship between the disorders.

For instance, a study of ADHD types in a sample of female twins suggested that oppositional defiance disorder (ODD, a disorder that involves excessive defiance of authority) is often comorbid with inattentive ADHD. There were several different categories of ADHD in this population: inattentive, inattentive with ODD, and combined type ADHD.[5] Other disorders, such as depression, often occur with or are mistaken for ADHD because they have similar or identical symptoms.

ADULT ADHD AND THE UTAH CRITERIA

ADHD used to be considered a disorder that affected only children up until their middle or late teens. More recent research has shown, however, that 30 percent to 70 percent of people with ADHD experience some symptoms of the disorder into their 20s and later. Since hyperactive type ADHD tends to occur in childhood and either develops into combined type ADHD or becomes less severe, it seems more cases of adult ADHD should be diagnosed as either combined type or inattentive type. Diagnostic criteria for ADHD were designed for a childhood disorder, however, so they do not always apply perfectly to ADHD symptoms in adults. As a result, the most commonly used list of criteria for adult ADHD requires both hyperactivity and problems with attention, so technically doctors only diagnose the combined type of ADHD in adults. The obvious hyperactivity common in children with ADHD is much more subtle in adults and tends to take the form of continuous feelings of physical edginess, restlessness, physical stress, and inability to relax.

Adult ADHD is considered a continuation of the childhood disorder, so a longstanding history of ADHD symptoms is an important aspect of diagnosing the adult form of the disorder. ADHD-like symptoms that have only recently appeared for an adult are not likely to indicate ADHD. A set of criteria, called the Utah criteria, were developed by Paul Wender help to bridge the gap between diagnostic criteria for childhood ADHD and the disorder as it appears in adults.[6] These criteria are quite restrictive, requiring not only a history of ADHD symptoms since childhood but also continuing problems due to hyperactivity and inattentiveness. In addition, at least two of the following symptoms must be present:

1. Rapid mood swings
2. Irritability and hot temper
3. Lack of ability to deal with stress
4. Disorganization
5. Impulsivity

These criteria shift emphasis to a person's emotional state and internal experience, making diagnosis more challenging, especially for nonspecialists. These criteria have been criticized for excluding primarily inattentive ADHD, which might be characterized by disorganization, excessive daydreaming, or inability to make or carry through decisions, but would not be related to hot temper, impulsivity, or other hyperactivity-related symptoms.[7]

Among adults who have continuing ADHD, disorganization continues to be a problem that affects work deadlines and social commitments, and organizing large projects into smaller goals and planning for long-term goals is difficult. At the same time, prioritizing important tasks is hard and priorities are often disorganized, leading to frustration on the part of the person with ADHD as well as those around them. Impulsiveness appears as difficulty refraining from blurting out socially inappropriate thoughts, especially insulting or rude ones, or as an inability to refrain from making impulsive purchases. The good news for adults with ADHD is that, while problems with the disorder can continue, the stimulant medications used to treat children continue to be effective for adults.

ICD-10

While the *DSM-IV* is the standard in the United States, the *International Classification of Diseases, Tenth Revision* (**ICD-10**) put out by the World Health Organization is the predominant standard in Western Europe. The *ICD-10* equivalent to ADHD is **hyperkinetic disorder**. Hyperkinetic is a synonym for hyperactive. Hyperkinetic disorder is relatively similar to combined type ADHD in that it requires both hyperactivity and inattention. From the *ICD-10* guidelines, hyperkinetic disorders are related to a "lack of persistence in activities that require cognitive involvement, and a tendency to move from one activity to another without completing any one, together with disorganized, ill-regulated, and excessive activity."

The *ICD-10*'s hyperkinetic disorder does not have a purely inattentive or purely hyperactive subtype. This probably contributes to the smaller number of people diagnosed with the disorder in Western Europe. The *ICD-10* criteria also recognize a hyperkinetic conduct disorder, which is simply the combination of hyperkinetic and **conduct disorder** criteria. A conduct disorder is repeated antisocial, aggressive, and/or defiant behavior.

DON'T GET STRUNG UP BY THE GUIDELINES

Resources like the *DSM* and the *ICD* are extremely valuable. They help standardize the ways in which psychologists and psychiatrists view disorders. (The *ICD* covers a wide spectrum of disorders, not only mental ones.) It is important to realize, however, that they are guidelines written by people at a particular time. As information on disorders changes, the thinking on classifying disorders changes as well. It is perhaps best to consider these guidelines a snapshot of the most popular views on a disorder at the time they were written. This is one of the major advantages of working with a specialist in a particular disorder. They are more likely to be up to date on the evolution of research and changing views in their specialty. Attention-deficit/hyperactivity disorder is a complex disorder, and defining a small number of subtypes for such a disorder is a difficult task. A small number of subtypes are unlikely to perfectly summarize the differences among people with ADHD when the disorder itself is likely to have different underlying genetic and environmental causes in different people.

3 Pay Attention! Neurobiology of Attention and ADHD

So, we were driving down Route 1, and my friend Mandy was *telling me about the cute guy who lives across the hall from her.* *He's studying to become a doctor or something. Route 1 at rush* *hour is such a pain. Just then my friend Jesse called on my cell. I* *fished it out of my purse, tossing things back in after I got the phone* *out. We figured out which movie we were going to go to and I held* *the phone against my chin to pull things back out of my purse* *until I found my pen and a ragged receipt from McDonald's to jot* *down the time for the movie. Mandy started talking about her cute* *neighbor again and I made "mmm hmm" noises as I put my phone* *and other things back. Slam! I hit the brakes, Mandy yelped, and* *my purse hit the floor spilling everything all over the front seat. I* *didn't quite stop in time, but I just tapped the bumper of the car* *ahead of me. Route 1 had turned into a parking lot while I was* *busy with other stuff. Fortunately there wasn't any damage besides* *a scratch on the other car's bumper, so I apologized a lot, we got* *each other's information, and got back in our cars. My heart is just* *now slowing down, though.*

An accident like that could happen to almost anyone. Even good drivers have days on which they overtax their ability to cope with distractions. It happens more often, however, to teenagers than people in their mid- to late 20s or older. Teens with ADHD are even more accident prone and have about twice as many accidents as teens without ADHD, probably

Figure 3.1 Psychologist William James, in his 1890 book *Principles of Psychology*, described children of "explosive will." *U.S. National Library of Medicine, National Institutes of Health*

because driving requires a certain level of sustained, focused attention.

The psychologist William James provided what is probably the most famous definition of attention in modern psychology in his 1890 book *Principles of Psychology*. (The full text of James' book is available online at http://psychclassics.yorku.ca/James/ Principles.) James said, "Everyone knows what attention is. It is the taking possession by the mind in clear and vivid form, of one out of what seem several simultaneously possible objects or trains of thought." In other words, to pay attention is to focus on one of many possibilities. As James put it, focusing our attention "implies withdrawal from some things in order to deal effectively with others."

ATTENTION OR INHIBITION?

While much of the focus of ADHD-related research has been on attention, there is another major school of thought on the causes of ADHD. Some researchers believe that the central, or core, deficit in ADHD is not actually attention but inhibitory control. Attention and inhibitory control are both considered executive functions—the functions in the brain responsible for overall control of conscious behavior and decision making. The classic analogy is an executive sitting at her desk in the front of the brain, making decisions about what to pay attention to, which activities to inhibit or allow, or where to eat lunch. Anyone who has ever sat in class and resisted the urge to jump up and run around the hall or kick the desk of the person in front of them, or to pull out the book they've been reading and ignore the class, has done so thanks to their brain's executive functions.

In the model of ADHD with inhibitory control as the core deficit, a lack of inhibition causes the other deficits such as hyperactivity or inattention. In other words, when inhibitory control is working correctly, one's attention does not wander because it is inhibited from doing so. An originator of this view, Russell Barkley, says that "Even what we call problems with attention seem to be problems with inhibition—

inhibiting the urge to do something a child would rather be doing than the task at hand."[8] For example, it is possible, and even easy, for many people with ADHD to pay attention to interesting, high-stimulation things like video games because less inhibitory control is required to keep their mind from wandering away from these desirable, fun activities than for less-engaging activities, like geometry class. Hyperactivity, when present, happens because there is not enough inhibitory control to keep a person focused on a single task and help the person hold still.

In the theory of ADHD where attention is thought to be the core deficit, attention is hard to sustain in the absence of high stimulation. Unless an activity is very fun or interesting, the mind does not stay on track, so the person's attention wanders to something new, giving the appearance of a lack of inhibitory control. It is very difficult to disentangle these executive functions because, as William James pointed out, attention to one thing is related to excluding our attention from others.

A BRIEF HISTORY OF ATTENTION

In the years between James' observations and this book, researchers have paid a great deal of attention to the topic of attention. Until the 1950s, most of the research on attention was based on **introspection**, or researchers "looking within" their own experiences. Conclusions from this kind of study are often specific to each person, and it is very difficult to decide which conclusion is correct when one person's introspection differs from another's. Attention was a popular subject for introspection, and Sigmund Freud was one of the well-known thinkers who contemplated its workings in the human brain.

Between the 1950s and the present day, attention has also received a great deal of study. The nature of the study shifted, however, from introspection to designing experiments to test aspects of attention in controlled situations. Many of these experiments involve ways in which attention can be split between different kinds of details. For instance, one experiment placed random objects in a box, which was then observed for a limited time by volunteers. The volunteers were then asked to identify or describe the objects, and researchers found out that the objects most unfamiliar to the observer were the best-remembered objects. This experiment suggests that attention goes to things that are novel.

Magnetic Resonance Imaging (MRI)

MRI is a valuable technique for looking inside living tissue, which makes it incredibly useful for looking at brain structures in living patients. In medicine it is most often used to look for tumors or other changes in normal tissue that might indicate illness. For ADHD researchers, MRI images of the brain can be used to calculate the sizes (volumes) of different parts of the brain. Many of the studies discussed in this book used MRI to investigate the sizes of brain regions in living people.

The mechanism of MRI is rather complicated. A series of very strong magnetic pulses are passed through the person whose body is being imaged at different angles. This is often done in three dimensions at 90° from each other (think about the corner of a cube). Information from the three signals is combined into information about small cubes, or voxels (the equivalent of a pixel on your computer screen, but 3-D instead of flat), that make up an MRI recording. Using special software, an image is reconstructed from the voxels. One common way of looking at this image is as a series of slices such as the one shown in

In addition to these indirect experiments with human volunteers, animal experiments—notably recording electrical signals from the brain, examining the effects of various drugs, and studying trained and untrained behavior—have also shed light on attention. New technology has provided new imaging techniques for medical use, especially magnetic resonance imaging (**MRI**). These have also been used to study the changes in the brain, called **neural correlates**, which occur along with changes in attention. (Anything related to the brain

Figure 3.2 These slices can be placed together to create fascinating ways of looking at anatomy.

A similar kind of MRI can be used to examine brain function. This type, known as a functional or fMRI, lets us visualize the amount of blood present in a tissue. Changes in the amount of blood often indicate activation of the tissue, especially in the brain. That is, active brain tissue requires more oxygen, and more blood flow is recruited to fill the requirement.

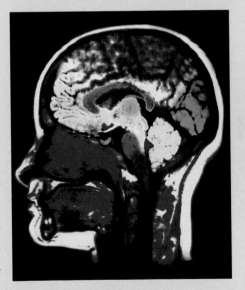

Figure 3.2 A computer-enhanced MRI scan of the brain. ADHD researchers can use MRI images to calculate the sizes of different parts of the brain. © *Scott Camazine & Sue Trainor/Photo Researchers, Inc.*

is "neural," and changes that occur along with other changes are called "correlates." If the size of part of the brain is larger in people with ADHD, for instance, this difference this would be a neural correlate of ADHD.) These techniques have also been used to study how differences in attention between people with and without ADHD are related to structure and function in the brain. Structural changes are differences in size or shape of parts of the brain in people with ADHD versus the general population. A larger or smaller size of a particular region of the brain can be a useful indication of a disorder. Likewise, functional brain studies can help to indicate changes in brain activity or function patterns that may be associated with ADHD.

NEUROTRANSMITTERS AND ADHD

The brain uses a variety of molecules to transmit signals between cells in the brain called **neurons**. These molecules are called **neurotransmitters**. There is strong evidence that changes in the parts of the brain related to the neurotransmitter **dopamine** are associated with ADHD. Dopamine has many functions in different parts of the brain, including a central function in the brain's reward and attention systems. Changes in a number of the genes in the dopamine system increase the risk of ADHD. Stimulants, the kind of medication most commonly given to people with ADHD, work on the dopamine system. **Norepinephrine**, another neurotransmitter in the brain with major roles in attention systems, is probably also involved in ADHD. Neurons that use this neurotransmitter are often found in the parts of the brain relating to attention, alertness, and decision making, such as the prefrontal cortex and striatum. One model of neurotransmitters in ADHD suggests that there is an imbalance of the activity of these two

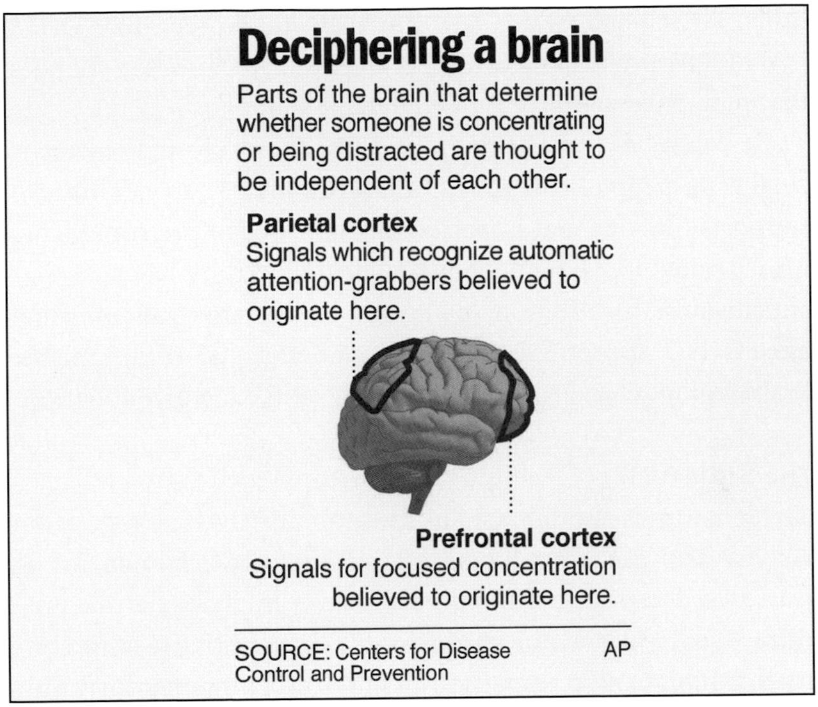

Deciphering a brain

Parts of the brain that determine whether someone is concentrating or being distracted are thought to be independent of each other.

Parietal cortex
Signals which recognize automatic attention-grabbers believed to originate here.

Prefrontal cortex
Signals for focused concentration believed to originate here.

SOURCE: Centers for Disease Control and Prevention   AP

Figure 3.3 Research has consistently found that the prefrontal cortex is smaller in people with ADHD than in other people. © *AP Images*

neurotransmitters in these areas—too little dopamine activity and too much norepinephrine activity.

THE PREFRONTAL CORTEX (PFC)

The prefrontal cortex is the region of the brain most closely associated with decision making and organization of priorities—often called executive function. Damage in different parts of the prefrontal cortex can cause problems with organization, planning, working memory, and stopping "improper" social behavior. It can also produce problems related to directing and stopping physical behaviors, often called motor or locomotor skills. These changes are very similar to those seen in ADHD, making the prefrontal cortex a prime place to look for changes that may cause symptoms of ADHD.

Research has consistently found that the prefrontal cortex is smaller in people with ADHD than in other people. This also supports the idea that impaired function in the prefrontal cortex is related to ADHD. Studies of neural activity reach similar conclusions. In addition, pathways of neurons called **neural circuits** link the prefrontal cortex with the striatum, another brain region related to decision-making and executive function.

THE STRIATUM

The striatum is another area of the brain involved in regulating activity and executive function. Scientists have known for at least two decades that in animals, lesions in the striatum produce ADHD-like symptoms including hyperactivity, poor ability to inhibit or stop responses, and poor working memory. This suggests that irregularities in the striatum may also be related to ADHD. The striatum also has a large number of neurons that use dopamine to communicate and is affected by dopamine-related drugs such as stimulants.

Most researchers who looked at the volume of the striatum found that, as in the prefrontal cortex, the volume is smaller in people with ADHD than people without the disorder. A smaller volume of striatum could indicate less ability to inhibit actions and perform the other tasks associated with the striatum. The striatum is divided into several smaller regions based on visual and cell type differences, and size differences in one of these regions, the caudate, are associated with ADHD at younger ages. The differences grow smaller with age and are much smaller in people with adult ADHD, however, suggesting one way in which childhood ADHD may change over a lifetime.[9]

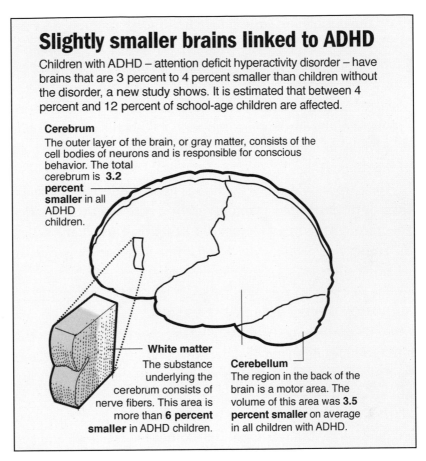

Slightly smaller brains linked to ADHD

Children with ADHD – attention deficit hyperactivity disorder – have brains that are 3 percent to 4 percent smaller than children without the disorder, a new study shows. It is estimated that between 4 percent and 12 percent of school-age children are affected.

Cerebrum
The outer layer of the brain, or gray matter, consists of the cell bodies of neurons and is responsible for conscious behavior. The total cerebrum is **3.2 percent smaller** in all ADHD children.

White matter
The substance underlying the cerebrum consists of nerve fibers. This area is more than **6 percent smaller** in ADHD children.

Cerebellum
The region in the back of the brain is a motor area. The volume of this area was **3.5 percent smaller** on average in all children with ADHD.

Figure 3.4 © *AP Images*

OTHER CHANGES IN THE BRAIN

Many researchers have studied the relationship between ADHD and changes in the frontal cortex and striatum. Attention-deficit/hyperactivity disorder is complex, however, and it shouldn't be too surprising to learn that researchers have found differences in a number of other parts of the brain as well. Two of these regions are the cerebellum and the corpus callosum, which both have lower volumes in people with ADHD, suggesting they also have less function. The cerebellum is the part of the brain responsible for putting together information on the perceptions of our senses and the physical actions of our muscles. Combining these two kinds of information allows the cerebellum to provide feedback that improves our fine motor skills and coordination. Some people with ADHD tend to have more problems with coordination and motor skills than people with no ADHD, so the cerebellum may be involved with this aspect of the disorder.

The corpus callosum is the bridge between the left and right sides of the brain. Most communication between the two sides goes through this brain region. The bridge is somewhat smaller, on average, in people with ADHD, but it is not clear exactly what the effect of this size difference might be.

ACTIVATION DIFFERENCES IN THE BRAIN

Most of the changes discussed above are differences in the size (volume) or shape of a part of the brain. There can also be differences in the function of a part of the brain that are not reflected in visible changes to the brain's structure. One kind of functional difference is a difference in activity. When a region of the brain is used, it becomes more active, and the body sends more blood to that region to provide oxygen and energy to support the activity. A functional MRI (fMRI) can measure how much blood is going to a given part of the brain. People with ADHD have less activity in the prefrontal cortex and the striatum than people with no ADHD, even when given tasks that challenge their executive function. Stimulants activate these regions, which may be how they improve the ability of people with ADHD to perform executive functions.

SEX DIFFERENCES AND BRAIN DIFFERENCES

Because ADHD is more commonly diagnosed in males, relatively few studies of the effects of ADHD on brain regions have included females. One large MRI study of brain differences that did include female subjects, however, observed similar fundamental differences in both male and female subjects with ADHD. This suggests that despite the differences in frequency of ADHD subtypes between males and females, there is more similarity than difference between sexes in the neurobiology of the disorder.

DIFFICULT TO PREDICT: A COMPLEX, HETEROGENEOUS DISORDER

ADHD is complex, so each person with ADHD may have a number of factors that contribute to their disorder. In addition, ADHD is heterogeneous, so a factor such as a change in brain structure responsible for a predisposition towards ADHD in one population may be entirely absent in another population that is also predisposed towards the disorder. Because of the complexity and heterogeneity of ADHD, it can be challenging to study the origins of the disorder in the brain because they may differ from person to person. For instance, researchers can say that there are regions of the brain, such as the striatum, where small size of the brain region is associated with ADHD in general, but they cannot predict that a particular person with a small striatum will have ADHD or that a person with a normal-sized striatum will not have ADHD.

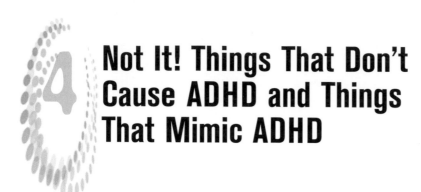

Not It! Things That Don't Cause ADHD and Things That Mimic ADHD

When Daria was younger, she was an active, friendly child, but as she neared age 13, she seemed more and more withdrawn and stopped paying attention to class work and assignments. Nothing really seemed to get through to her and she mostly wanted to be left alone. While she was not prone to anger, her moods and attitude were usually pretty negative. When a teacher, who only knew Daria from the current school year, suggested that Daria might have primarily inattentive ADHD, her parents made an appointment with a psychiatrist, who had a different story to tell.

According to her psychiatrist, Daria was depressed. Stimulant medications wouldn't have helped her and might have made her depression worse. Daria's psychiatrist prescribed her an antidepressant and, at the psychiatrist's suggestion, Daria's parents made weekly appointments for Daria with a therapist, but as the medicine kicked in they eventually stopped going and opted for regular check-ins with her psychiatrist. Daria's depression seemed to be mostly biological, and with regular tutoring and minimal help at organization, she was able to catch up in her work enough to advance with her classmates.

Tommy, on the other hand, was a terror. Anything his parents told him to do was automatically the last thing in the world he would consider. His teachers found him uncooperative too, and he often got detention after school for arguing with teachers

Figure 4.1 A child with ADHD acts out in front of his mother. © *Getty Images*

or fellow students or, on one occasion, just standing up and walking out of his English class. Tommy almost never finished his homework—he seemed to lose interest about a quarter of the way through—and he was behind in all his classes and had managed to alienate all his teachers.

Unfortunately, Tommy didn't want help of any kind. He was in an unusually good mood the first day he met with a counselor about his problem. The next time Tommy met with the counselor to start working with him, though, he wouldn't even come down from his room. Each time following, after a few minutes, Tommy simply stopped paying attention and then became angry and stormed off when his counselor tried to bring him back on track. Eventually, his parents and counselor agreed that Tommy needed more professional evaluation before academic and organizational tutoring would be helpful.

Tommy probably had oppositional defiant disorder (ODD), which is characterized by defiant behavior, especially toward parents and teachers. The twist here is that Tommy might also have had ADHD, because the disorders tend to occur together fairly often. Stimulant medications might have helped with Tommy's ADHD, but they probably wouldn't help with his ODD. They might even have made it worse. One of the difficulties with ADHD is that it can coexist with other psychiatric disorders. It takes an expert to properly evaluate what is going on with a particular person, and to organize the right medications and treatments when more than one disorder is present.

Psychiatric disorders and many other causes can result in hyperactive and impulsive behavior and a lack of attention, particularly in young children who naturally have a short attention span, so there are a number of real disorders that resemble ADHD. Similarly, environmental changes and influences, especially large and disruptive changes, can produce changes in behavior that look like ADHD. These similar symptoms with environmental causes are known as phenocopies. People, physicians and professionals included, have a strong tendency to try to find simple causes when something is going wrong, but it is important to consider the possibility that ADHD symptoms may be caused by the environment or similar disorders, or may be comorbid with other disorders.

ADHD IS SOMETIMES MISDIAGNOSED AS . . .

Oppositional Defiant Disorder. Oppositional behavior is a pattern of angry, argumentative behavior towards authority figures such as parents and teachers. It shows itself differently at different ages, and as with ADHD, the disorder is the extreme of the normal range of human behavior. From time to time, everyone is oppositional towards authority, particularly when tired, hungry, upset at something or someone, or simply stressed from the demands of life. This is particularly true of younger children who have fewer social barriers between feelings and behaviors.

The key to recognizing ODD is that it is a persistent and unreasonable level of defiant and oppositional behavior. The key to distinguishing it from ADHD is that hyperactivity and distractibility will not be nearly as clear when there is less authority to rebel against. Distinguishing the two can still be more difficult than it sounds, especially since ODD is often comorbid with ADHD. One feature of ADHD is particular difficulty in concentrating on tasks like homework or schoolwork, and the efforts of authority figures (sometimes a bit unwelcome) are often needed to help with maintaining focus. In these circumstances, it can be hard to figure out whether oppositional behavior is due to ODD or to an unusual aversion to doing homework brought on by ADHD. Sometimes it is easier to distinguish ODD by focusing on reactions to activities that are neutral or pleasant, like game playing. People with ADHD may find it difficult to finish games but will typically be less oppositional when the idea of playing games is brought up by an authority figure.

A Learning Disorder. Attention-deficit/hyperactivity disorder is not usually thought of as a learning disorder (LD) itself, though a person with ADHD is twice as likely to have a learning disorder.[10] A learning disorder directly and primarily affects a process typically involved in learning, such as a reading disability or trouble recognizing the phonemes, or sounds, that make up words. The idea that ADHD is not a learning disorder has recently become somewhat more controversial, since ADHD can directly affect the capacity of students to pay attention in the classroom. In addition, ADHD is most often noticed in its effects on working in the classroom and doing homework.

It is easy to mistake ADHD for a learning disorder, and vice versa, because they both often result in a student failing to pay attention to their work. Of course, there are many reasons that students don't pay attention to their class work. Daria, for instance, was depressed. The trick is to figure out why a particular student isn't paying attention to their work. In the case of a learning disorder, it is usually because the disorder is making the material hard to understand. Imagine how hard it would be to pay attention to this book if someone rearranged some words even just a little. *A reader oulwd find ti difultfic to peek on eadring if it weer a struggle to edal with verye sentence.* Eventually the reader would become frustrated, stop paying attention to the book, and instead get up and walk around or try to pay attention to things that were more fun or comprehensible. If someone tried to make this person sit down and read the book again, he might try for a few minutes before his attention wandered again. To a person who didn't know he was having trouble reading, this would look a lot like ADHD. When both might be present in one person, it's usually best to work on helping the learning disorder first, to see if that improves the ADHD-like symptoms.

Depression. Depression is quite different from learning disorders and from ADHD, but a depressed person often finds it very difficult to stay motivated, so their attention tends to wander. Unlike someone with a learning disorder, a depressed person probably won't respond in an agitated way when they stop paying attention to work. Instead, they may appear to be a bit spacey or vacant. When depression is mistaken for ADHD, it is usually mistaken for the primarily inattentive subtype of ADHD. It is particularly bad when depression is misdiagnosed as ADHD, because the stimulant medications so often prescribed for ADHD can actually worsen depression.

Since some antidepressants are also helpful for ADHD, it's important to work with a psychiatrist with some experience with both disorders. It may be possible to use bupropion (Wellbutrin) or some other medication to help with both disorders. If not, it is usually best to treat the depression first and then work on the ADHD.

ADHD IS NOT CAUSED BY . . .

It is very hard to prove a negative, especially with a complex disorder like ADHD that is undoubtedly affected by the environment. Generally, the best that scientists can do is establish that, most of the time, one thing is not related to another—for example, ADHD and diet. This is because an experiment can fail to support a theory for quite a number of reasons besides the theory being wrong. For instance, an experiment could be flawed or it might not have enough **power** to detect a difference. Thus, to be accurate, scientists say that there is no evidence that certain things cause ADHD. There is evidence, however, that solidly suggests that ADHD is usually related to abnormalities in the brain that are mostly influenced by genetics, though they may show up in different ways depending on differences in the environment.

Too much sugar. One of the most common popular theories about ADHD is that it is related to a number of possible dietary issues and that adding something to a diet or taking something away will "fix" ADHD. Diet and behavior are certainly related—oatmeal for breakfast, for example, is associated with better performance on tests of learning and memory than prepared cereal or no breakfast[11]—but ADHD is not a primarily dietary disorder. Yet many dietary changes have been prescribed over the past 30 years for ADHD. The most common idea is that too much sugar causes ADHD, and that ADHD can be treated by decreasing sugar consumption. This is based on the commonly held wisdom that sugar causes hyperactivity. While this seems anecdotally true to

Do You Have the Power?

It is very difficult to prove a negative. Generally rather than saying "X is not related to Y," scientists will say, "There is no evidence to support a relationship between X and Y." The difference between these two statements is subtle but important. Doing an experiment to get results is important, but interpreting the results carefully and correctly is even more important. If scientists find a result, that's great! Everything is simple—they found the result and it's significant. When they do an experiment and don't find a result, understanding the meaning of the experiment is harder.

Saying that the data doesn't support a relationship implies that scientists have planned an experiment that is likely to detect the kind of relationship they are expecting. In other words, they have an idea of the power of the experiment to detect a relationship of a given strength. If a researcher collects a small sample of data and then fails to find a weak relationship, it shouldn't be surprising. When looking at an experiment, scientists should always ask how big they expect the effect will be and how surprised they should be if they fail to find a result.

For instance, there is very strong evidence that men are, in general, taller than women. If three men and three women are picked at random, however, three tall women and three short men may be chosen. In this case, the data don't support the idea that men are taller than women, but because only a few men and women were chosen for the experiment it is not very surprising that the expected relationship was not found because the experiment had very little power. If the experiment involved 1,000 men and 1,000 women, however, it would be very surprising not to find that men are taller than women on average because the experiment had lots of power to detect the size difference.

many people, it does not seem to be the case in children with or without ADHD.

In an excellent review, "Sugar and the Hyperactive Child," in the *New England Journal of Medicine*, Marcel Kinsbourne describes a variety of studies of the topic.[12] It is important that studies of this sort be **blinded** (conducted so that the subjects judging the child's behavior do not know whether the child has been given sugar or not) and **controlled** (conducted so that some children are given sugar and some children are not given sugar). Studies that are not controlled are thus subject to the **placebo effect.** This means that people tend to see effects where they believe there should be effects. In the case of sugar and hyperactivity, most people believe there is a link between the two, so when they know that a child has been given sugar, they are inclined to believe the child will be more hyperactive. Studies subject to the placebo effect tend to show that sugar has an effect on hyperactivity, while studies that are controlled are more complicated. Usually, controlled studies show no effect of sugar on activity level, though one study done in 1980 suggested that sugar might increase aggressiveness but not activity level in hyperactive children.[13] Kinsbourne summarizes the scientific evidence on this controversy, saying that, "Given the largely negative findings and the failure of the occasional significant outcome to be confirmed in subsequent studies, it appears that any adverse effect of sugar is by no means as severe or as prevalent as uncontrolled observation and opinion would suggest. Specifically, there is no evidence that sugar alone can turn a child with normal attention into a hyperactive child."

This review was an introduction to an article in the same issue of the *New England Journal of Medicine* describing controlled experiments that detected little difference in behavior between experimental diets high in sucrose (sugar), aspartame (the sweetener in NutraSweet), and saccharine (another artificial sweetener).[14] These two papers caused a flood of letters to the editor from doctors and researchers, showing how controversial it was to conclude that sugar is not strongly related to hyperactivity. One of the more interesting objections raised by several people who wrote letters was that high-sugar diets are also likely to be low in nutrients, and that the effects of sugar in real world situations might be indirectly due to the lack of nutrients, which would be harder to see in a diet where the amount of sugar is being varied but the amount of nutrients is being kept as constant as possible.

While adding sugar to a diet does not seem sufficient to cause ADHD, Dr. Bart Hoebel's lab at Princeton University found that, in rats at least, sugar dependency is associated with greater sensitivity to amphetamine, a type of stimulant drug.[15] Sugar dependency is caused by allowing the rats to binge on sugar for a short time, denying them sugar for a period of time, and repeating this pattern for a number of cycles. The researchers found that changes due to sugar dependency in rats are remarkably similar to changes that happen when rats are introduced to and become addicted to drugs of abuse. They hypothesize that sugar dependency may cause long-term changes in the dopamine system, which is involved in the response to stimulants and believed to be involved in ADHD.

Is this a muddy picture? Unfortunately, many pictures in science are a little muddy, and an important part of being a scientist is sorting out a consistent story from confusing results. This often requires reading as much as possible to see what many different people have to say on a subject.

Allergies, especially to additives and preservatives. Allergies and sensitivity to many foods have been and continue to be proposed as a cause of primarily hyperactive ADHD, but studies have generally been negative. Allergies are reactions of the immune system to substances in the environment called *allergens.* The allergens most commonly thought to cause ADHD are food additives and preservatives, though other substances have been proposed.

The idea that allergies or sensitivities to food additives and preservatives cause ADHD is based on claims popularized by Dr. Benjamin Feingold in the 1970s, and it has become much less popular since that time. Dr. Feingold proposed the **Feingold diet** as a treatment for ADHD. A 1983 analysis of 23 studies of the Feingold diet concluded that it was not effective in treating ADHD, though similar studies of ADHD and potential allergens have continued since then.[16] One objection that has been raised to some of the studies is that they tend to use a lower dose of additives and preservatives than is encountered in daily life, and indeed some studies that have found effects of additives on ADHD symptoms have been high-dose studies.[17]

The general idea that ADHD results from a **food allergy** is still quite common in the popular press, though many study results are negative, including results from a large study of 312 children referred to an allergist. This 1998 study found no association between the results of medical tests for allergies and a survey that measures parents' reports about their children's ability to pay attention. Almost all studies that looked at medical tests for allergic reactions showed little association with ADHD symptoms, while studies that examined the relationship between allergy-related symptoms and ADHD symptoms seemed somewhat more likely to be positive. This suggests that allergy symptoms (runny nose, skin rash, and scratchy eyes, for instance) may be more related to ADHD symptoms than medical tests indicating that a person has an allergy.

One controlled study, for instance, reported that atopic eczema, an irritation of the skin due to allergies, was related to hyperactivity.[18] Another group in a smaller, less controlled study, found an association between ADHD-like symptoms and allergic rhinitis—the stuffy or runny nose associated with aller-gies.[19] They hypothesized that sleep disturbances caused by the rhinitis might cause ADHD symptoms or make them worse.

Nutrient deficiencies. There is not much evidence for many of the nutritional deficiencies that people have thought might be related to ADHD. There is, however, some evidence that omega-3 (an essential fatty acid common in fish oil) or other essential fatty acids may be somehow related to ADHD, though there are also studies that show no relationships.

There are several studies that suggest a role for zinc in ADHD, but many of the positive studies of zinc as a treatment for ADHD, or at least as a nutrient linked to ADHD, have been performed in countries other than the United States. In the United States and western Europe, zinc deficiencies are not very common, suggesting that zinc may be more important for ADHD in some regions of the world than others. Recently, how-ever, a study in the United States suggested a role for zinc levels in primarily inattentive ADHD, but not hyperactive ADHD.[20]

While a few nutrient deficiencies might be able to make ADHD symptoms stronger, the majority of foods and nutri-ents are relatively neutral with respect to ADHD symptoms. Another take on the idea of dietary deficiencies is the idea that ADHD can be treated using high doses of vitamins. This idea, called **megavitamin therapy**, is another once-popular belief that has become considerably less popular over time. It is worth mentioning because megavitamin therapy can be dangerous if fat-soluble vitamins are included. These vitamins can build up to toxic levels in the body if taken in large doses. It is important to consult a doctor before taking large doses of any vitamin. Here the indications from the scientific literature are clear. Megavitamin therapy doesn't work,[21] and in one study the group taking vitamins had significantly worse symptoms than the than placebo group.[22]

A yeast or other infection. Another theory is that ADHD and a variety of other disorders are due to an overgrowth of yeast in the digestive tract and/or skin. This hypothesized overgrowth is often called systemic candidiasis after the scientific name of the yeast, *Candida,* that is believed to cause the disorder. This idea was first proposed in the 1980s by a pediatrician, Dr. William Crook, in his book *The Yeast Connection,* and has been popularized in a number of books since then. The idea is that the toxins released by the yeast weaken the immune system and more directly affect other parts of the body. Despite its popularity, however, there is virtually nothing in the medical literature about this hypothesis, a situation that is often the case when a hypothesis originates apart from the medical thinking about a disorder.

Candida overgrowth does happen in humans, where it usually manifests itself in women as a vaginal yeast infection, easily treated with antifungal drugs. Antibiotic use can also promote yeast infections, since it kills bacteria that normally check the growth of the yeast. Other *Candida* overgrowths, however, are usually associated with compromised immune systems—for instance, oral thrush, an overgrowth of *Candida* in the mouth, which occurs in patients with symptomatic AIDS or other disorders that distress the immune system. These overgrowths are very seldom found in people with a healthy, intact immune system, and there is no association between ADHD and weakened immune systems.

Dr. Crook's treatment for systemic yeast overgrowth is elimination of all sugar and foods made with molds and yeast (including bread), and reducing additives and allergens, similar to the elimination diets described above, but with the possible addition of antifungal drugs to combat the hypothesized ongoing infection. This method has not been studied in a controlled test. The dietary changes are likely to have effects similar to the other diets described—that is, relatively minimal effects on attention.

Watching television / playing video games / using the computer. People with ADHD are probably not reading this book, if they can help it, and are very unlikely to be reading it all the way through. People with ADHD tend to read less and consume multimedia entertainment more. This is probably because multimedia entertainment requires a shorter attention span to create reward. A novel may be boring for the first 10 pages, while characters are introduced and plot points are set up. A person with a normal attention span will generally push through this boring section, while someone with ADHD will often give up and do something more immediately rewarding like watching television. The great thing about TV is that a whole plot can be fit into half an hour or so. Likewise, video games and using the computer have relatively quick rewards. These points were made with considerable force after a 2004 paper in the journal *Pediatrics* suggested that more frequent TV viewing before age seven is associated with attention difficulties at age seven.[23] It is very difficult to tell the chicken from the egg—does watching television promote ADHD or does ADHD promote watching television because children with ADHD want to watch more TV, because they are more likely to frustrate their parents and be sent off to watch TV, or even because interpersonal interactions are more challenging?

It is interesting, however, that a number of the letters to the editor of *Pediatrics* said something to the effect of "TV may well be a problem, but this report doesn't prove it." There is no solid, convincing evidence to support the idea that watching TV causes ADHD in otherwise normal individuals, but the belief that TV causes problems is quite widespread. Television may affect willingness to attempt tasks that are not as immediately rewarding, at least in children without ADHD, and be even more appealing

Figure 4.2 A 2004 paper in the journal *Pediatrics* suggested that more frequent TV viewing before age seven is associated with attention difficulties at age seven. © *Getty Images*

to children with ADHD. Since ADHD seems to have a very large genetic and early developmental component, however, watching television is unlikely to be a very large contributor.

Poor parenting. "Control your kids" is a refrain that parents of children with ADHD very quickly grow tired of hearing. Is

ADHD simply a matter of parents who are too lenient? There appear to be no studies that support this idea, but there is a confusing issue here. Families of children with ADHD do tend to be more disorganized, stressed, and chaotic than other families. Since ADHD has a large genetic component, this could be related to ADHD in one or both of the parents, which can have a tendency to produce a chaotic environment. As any parent knows, however, raising a child is itself chaotic and stressful, and raising a child with ADHD can be even more so.

Famous People with ADHD

Attention-deficit/hyperactivity disorder has been attributed to a large number of famous people, and indeed it seems that many of the geniuses in invention, politics, acting, and other fields have inexhaustible energy and a tendency to start many projects. Many also had difficulty early on in school and other characteristics of ADHD. Albert Einstein, Robin Williams, Thomas Edison, Leonardo da Vinci, Nicola Tesla, Frank Lloyd Wright, Howard Stern, Napoleon Bonaparte, and John F. Kennedy are only a small selection of people whose possible ADHD is a matter of much speculation.

Of course, it is much more difficult to actually confirm that someone has ADHD, and nearly impossible for historical figures. The problem is that many disorders resemble ADHD. Bipolar disorder, for instance, can look very similar to ADHD in its manic phase, as can other disorders discussed in this chapter, while difficulties in school can be caused by a nearly infinite number of circumstances. One of the few reliable reports of an ADHD diagnosis of a current celebrity is Jack Osbourne, who as of the referenced article was dubious of his diagnosis.[24]

The various disorders, especially oppositional defiant disorder (ODD), that often occur with ADHD also add a level of confusion to the picture. Oppositional defiant disorder causes stress between parents and children very directly, especially stress that shows up as conflict and negative interactions between parents and children. For instance, researchers examined the interactions of mothers and sons in three groups:

1. ADHD with no ODD
2. ADHD as well as ODD
3. No ADHD or ODD

The interactions of mothers and sons with ADHD were very similar to those of mothers and sons without ADHD. Only the interactions of mothers and sons with ADHD and ODD were different. These interactions included stricter rules and stronger reactions to misbehavior. Since these interactions often take the form of the child disobeying parental commands and opposing parental authority to an extreme extent, they probably contribute heavily to the idea that ADHD is caused by poor parenting skills.

5 Genes and Environment in ADHD

The earliest observations of ADHD-like behavior and the earliest theories about ADHD are all related to brain injury. This historical origin of the idea persisted for many years through terms for the disorder like *minimal brain injury* and *minimal brain damage*. While brain injuries can certainly result in ADHD symptoms, most people with ADHD have never had any brain injury, so in most cases the origin of the disorder lies elsewhere.

ADHD HAS A STRONG GENETIC COMPONENT
If brain injury does not cause most ADHD, what does? There are two major possibilities. The first is that ADHD is largely environmental and the second is that it is largely genetic. A first step to answering this question is to compare the frequency with which **monozygotic twins** (identical twins) are **concordant** for the disorder with the frequency with which **dizygotic twins** (fraternal or nonidentical twins) are concordant. The reason comparing identical and fraternal twins is such a useful approach is that the biggest thing that varies between the two types of twins is the amount of genetic material they have in common. Identical twins share almost 100 percent of their genetic material, while fraternal twins share 50 percent, exactly as much as an ordinary brother and sister. Both types of twins also share a very similar environment.

When one identical twin has ADHD, the other has it up to 92 percent of the time. Other studies give lower numbers but they are all higher than the rate at which fraternal twins have the disorder in common, which is a maximum of 36 percent. Overall, about half to three-quarters of the variability in ADHD traits is genetic, which means that genetics is usually more important than environment in determining who gets ADHD.

ADHD IS A COMPLEX TRAIT AFFECTED BY MULTIPLE GENES AND THE ENVIRONMENT

Disorders are almost always caused by a combination of genes, called the **genotype** (G), environment (E), and the way the genes interact with the environment (GxE). If we make a mathematical equation out of this relationship, with the disorder ADHD being the **phenotype** (P), it will look very simple, like this:

$$P = G + E + GxE$$

Some disorders have only one genetic cause and little environmental variation. These disorders are known as simple or **Mendelian disorders**, after the monk Gregor Mendel, who described inheritance of single-gene genetic traits. The classic example is Huntington's disease, which is caused by a single faulty gene that permits damage to the cerebral cortex. While the cause is simple, the symptoms are complex, worsening from involuntary twitches to eventual death. Such disorders are usually almost entirely genetically determined and are only affected by a single gene. Environmental influence in the development of simple diseases is fairly small and can be ignored as can the interaction of genes and environment. This simplifies the equation to P = G.

ADHD, like many common disorders such as heart disease and high blood pressure, as well as almost all psychological

Of course, one problem with this sort of study is that if only certain kinds of genes are looked for, only certain kinds will be found. Such a study works best when the systems underlying a disorder are at least somewhat understood. In the case of ADHD, many of the drugs known to affect the disorder are known to affect the pathways for dopamine (for instance, amphetamine and methylphenidate) and norepinephrine (for instance, atomoxetine and bupropion). Researchers have examined genes associated with these neurotransmitters fairly extensively, and have found a number of genes associated with ADHD. These observations mesh well with the regions of the brain that are thought to be most involved with attention and ADHD, as identified by brain imaging studies.

Several genes with strong evidence of involvement in ADHD are part of the system that regulates the amount of dopamine available in the brain. One of these genes is even targeted by some stimulant medications used to treat ADHD. The protein generated by this gene is known as the dopamine **transporter** because it removes dopamine from the space between neurons, called the **synapse** (Figure 5.1). People with ADHD sometimes have more dopamine transporters than people without ADHD have. This causes dopamine to be removed from the synapse too quickly, so there is less of it in the synapse than usual. Some other genes associated with ADHD include genes that code for proteins called **receptors,** which respond to the amount of dopamine in the brain. A form of the receptor associated with ADHD reduces the response to dopamine, so that the brain needs more dopamine to respond to anything. Faster removal of dopamine by the transporter and reduced response by the receptor both mean that more dopamine is needed. Stimulants increase the amount of dopamine in the synapse, making up for this lack. Changes in the gene that converts dopamine into norepinephrine are also associated with people with ADHD.

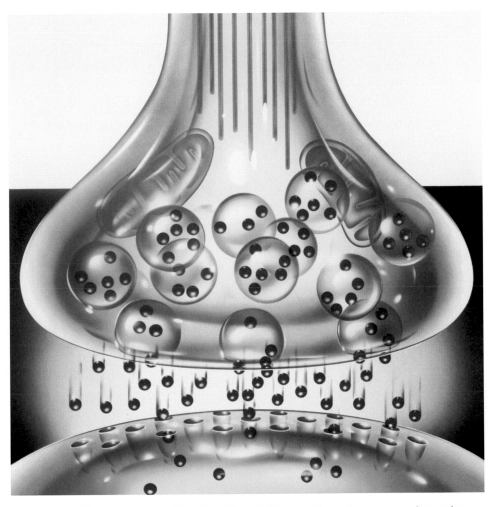

Figure 5.1 Nerve synapse. People with ADHD sometimes have more dopamine transporters than people without ADHD. This causes dopamine to be removed from the synapse too quickly, so there is less of it in the synapse than usual. © *John Bavosi/Photo Researchers, Inc.*

While the involvement of serotonin in ADHD is less well understood than that of dopamine and norepinephrine, it is clear that there is a connection. For instance, one type of medication used to treat ADHD (desipramine and imipramine are two examples of this kind of medication) keeps serotonin as well norepinephrine from being removed from the synapse. There are also serotonin-related genes that code for a transporter and receptors, respectively. Following a similar theme, variations in the molecular machinery involved in making dopamine and norepinephrine available in the brain are associated with ADHD. Mice lacking a gene involved in this process are hyperactive, and their hyperactivity can be treated with stimulants.

The theme connecting all of these genes is neurotransmitter release into and removal from the synapse, especially release and removal of dopamine and norepinephrine. It is likely that other genes involved in these systems and related to ADHD will be found, and it is also likely that other approaches, such as linkage analysis, a means of searching for genes related to a trait, will reveal other potential candidates and possibly even other mechanisms associated with ADHD.

Linkage Analysis

One way to study genetic disorders like ADHD is to investigate the relationship of particular genes with the disorder. This is very helpful if scientists already have a gene in mind, but is much harder if they don't know what genes to look at. There is a method, called linkage analysis, which can help. This method looks at many spots on different chromosomes, called markers (often there are more than 500,000 of them). If a marker is near a gene that affects ADHD, then one form of the marker may be inherited along with the gene and be more common among people with severe ADHD.

ADHD AND THE ENVIRONMENT

While ADHD has a large genetic component, environmental influences still clearly play a role. Some environmental influences, such as particular foods or food additives, that have been suggested in the popular press as causes for ADHD are fairly clearly not part of the environmental influence on ADHD. Convincing evidence for dietary influences on ADHD is lacking. In fact, most of the environmental influences on ADHD—with the exception of early lead exposure, which can occasionally be associated with development of ADHD symptoms—are influences on the environment in the womb during early development, suggesting that environmental effects on susceptibility to ADHD mostly occur before birth. Other environmental factors after birth, including injury to the brain, can increase the likelihood of ADHD, but these are not usually part of the cause of the disorder.

PROBLEMS IN PREGNANCY

Environmental risk factors during pregnancy, except for smoking, often seem to be related to **hypoxia**, or lack of oxygen to the fetus. Older age of the mother is also a risk factor during pregnancy, though this may also indirectly be related to hypoxia. Hypoxia can occur when there are complications during the pregnancy or during birth. One such risk factor is pregnancy-induced hypertension (high blood pressure), also called *toxemia* or *preeclampsia*. Pregnancy sometimes increases the mother's blood pressure sharply, which can be related to problems with the placenta and can result in poor blood supply to the baby. Since oxygen is carried to the baby via the blood, this can result in hypoxia. Since the age of the mother is related to risk for toxemia, this may be why older age of the mother is associated with ADHD. Long labor and extended delivery complications also increase the risk of hypoxia and are associated with ADHD. Premature birth is associated with ADHD as well, though premature births are not necessarily associated with damage due to hypoxia.

While the exact structures in the brain that are affected by hypoxia and may influence the development of ADHD are not known, one excellent candidate is the basal ganglia. The basal ganglia is a group of structures in the brain that connect several other brain regions and are related to executive function, motor responses, and learning, functions often impacted in ADHD. Since the basal ganglia is a very active region of the brain, especially during development, it is likely to be particularly sensitive to a lack of oxygen.

Smoking and drinking during pregnancy are additional risk factors for ADHD. Evidence for the impact of smoking on the risk for ADHD is particularly well documented. Studies have shown that mothers who smoked frequently during pregnancy were more likely to have children with ADHD. Studies also demonstrated that pregnant mice exposed to nicotine, the active ingredient in cigarettes, were more likely to have hyperactive offspring. Nicotine binds to receptors in the brain that indirectly affect the activity of the dopamine system. In other words, smoking while pregnant might affect how the baby's dopamine system forms, changing it permanently.

The effect of alcohol is probably less direct. Exposure to alcohol affects the fetus in many ways, which can present themselves in ADHD-like symptoms or a variety of other problems. Children with ADHD are more likely than children without ADHD to have been frequently exposed to alcohol in the womb, but whether the underlying effect of alcohol on the brain is similar to other environmental factors that contribute to ADHD is still an open question.

PROBLEMS IN THE HOME?

While poor parenting is very unlikely to cause ADHD, the disorder is correlated with problems or stresses in the family, including parental discord, criminal behavior (especially on the part of the father), mental disorders (especially on the part of the mother), and foster placement. The difficulty in interpreting these results comes from the strong heritability of ADHD. If one of the parents has the disorder, parental discord is likely to be more severe and all the problems related to parental discord are more likely to occur. For instance, if the father has untreated hyperactive/impulsive ADHD, his disorder also increases the likelihood that he will engage in criminal behavior, so problems in the home relating to his criminal behavior may really be an indirect effect of the genetic component of his ADHD. Likewise depression, one of the most common mental disorders in women, makes it more difficult for mothers to tolerate ADHD traits in their children, so may make it more likely that a child will be taken to the doctor for diagnosis. These environmental "risk factors" may actually be related to the genetics or identification of ADHD, rather than actually changing the intrinsic riskiness of the environment for development of ADHD symptoms.

CONCLUSIONS

Attention-deficit/hyperactivity disorder is a very heritable, complex disorder with a large genetic component. The known, clear environmental risk factors for the disorder tend to occur during pregnancy, though environment after birth undoubtedly plays a role in how ADHD is expressed and handled. The high heritability and evidence for environmental risk factors during pregnancy as well as the more conflicting and weaker evidence for later environmental risk factors such as diet suggests that ADHD is largely a disorder of the developing brain.

6 ADHD Medications

Jason was a fairly typical 13-year-old with primarily hyperactive/ impulsive ADHD. As he moved into a large junior high school from a small, well-structured elementary school, his restlessness and difficulty concentrating began to catch up with his school-work. On several occasions, Jason's teachers had discussed with his parents the possibility that he had ADHD, but because of his intelligence and relatively mild symptoms, the actual diagnosis had never been made. Jason was clearly having some severe problems, though, and by the time he was diagnosed, he was failing or almost failing several classes. Jason's parents arranged for him to see a psychiatrist, who suggested that Jason might have ADHD. After talking with his teachers and the school guidance counselor, his parents decided that the psychiatrist might be right and agreed to try medication.

Jason's psychiatrist started him on a moderate dose of a stimulant called Ritalin. He and his parents saw almost immediate improvement. Unfortunately, the Ritalin also made Jason a bit irritable and gave him a minor **facial tic**. Minor tics occur in 15 percent to 30 percent of people starting out on stimulant medication, but they usually go away on their own or when the amount of medication is lowered. Knowing this, Jason's psychiatrist cut back on his medicine a little at a time to see if that might help, but the tic wouldn't go away, at least while the dose was high enough to help Jason focus. Fortunately for

Jason, there are a number of medications that can help with ADHD. His doctor recommended Dexedrine, another stimulant medication, and Jason found that it helped him focus without producing any tics. With tutoring four times a week Jason was able to catch up with his class and stay caught up.

It was very important to Jason to know that he had options, especially after the first medication had unpleasant side effects. If Dexedrine had not worked, Jason's doctor could have tried a number of other medications, stimulant and nonstimulant. Different medications produce different side effects in different people, and what worked for Jason could produce unwanted side effects in someone else. Jason and his parents handled his diagnosis very well. They recognized that intensive effort was needed to correct his problems at school and that a long-term approach was important to help keep Jason on the right track. Jason's support team included his parents, his psychiatrist, his tutor, and a therapist with experience in counseling teenagers with ADHD. Studies have shown that medication alone is more successful than therapy alone in treating ADHD, but that both together are the best solution. Jason's therapist helped him to manage his emotions about ADHD, taking medication, and the usual problems that go with being a teenager—all of which can be made much harder by ADHD.

STIMULANTS FOR HYPERACTIVITY?

Stimulants are the **first-line** drug treatment for ADHD. This may seem surprising at first. Stimulants are drugs that increase activity in the **sympathetic nervous system** and at high doses can produce **euphoria** and increased physical activity levels. At these doses they are sometimes abused as recreational drugs, and can be very addictive, which is why these types of ADHD medication are **controlled substances** in the United States and elsewhere. Why would a stimulant help someone with ADHD?

It would seem that a drug that raises activity levels would be the last thing that would help ADHD, especially primarily hyperactive ADHD.

In 1937, Charles Bradley discovered that low doses of a stimulant known as Benzedrine, which was commonly used as an antihistamine to treat colds and asthma, helped his patients to focus. Benzedrine is a kind of stimulant called an amphetamine—a mix of two amphetamines, actually (levoamphetamine and dextroamphetamine, often written *l-amphetamine* and *d-amphetamine*). While there have been many changes in the medications available for ADHD in recent years, the first-line medication for ADHD is still low doses of stimulants—generally variations on amphetamines and methylphenidate, another kind of fast-acting stimulant with effects lasting only a few hours.

Stimulants have a variety of effects at high doses, but are believed to increase alertness and focus at both low and high doses. There is still some debate on this point. Some researchers believe that stimulants only increase focus at low and moderate doses and eventually decrease focus as they are taken in higher doses. At the low doses used to treat ADHD, however, stimulants definitely increase focus but do not cause euphoria and are not addictive.

It used to be popularly believed that low doses of stimulants only increase focus in people with ADHD, and that, in others, stimulants would reduce focus and perhaps produce higher levels of physical activity and euphoria. While low-dose stimulants produce more impressive behavioral changes in people with ADHD, they actually have similar effects in ADHD and non-ADHD brains.

MEDICINE OR BEHAVIOR

A large treatment study, the Multimodal Treatment Study of ADHD (MTA), showed that intensive **behavioral treatment** by itself is an effective treatment for ADHD, though not as effective as stimulant medication alone in changing ADHD symptoms. Interestingly, however, parents had a higher opinion of the effect of behavioral treatment, which could be due either to their values as to what was important as an outcome for ADHD treatment or their dissatisfaction with the idea of medication. The MTA also suggested that combining behavioral treatment with stimulant medication was more effective than using either one alone, so the best answer so far to the question of treatment through medication or behavior modification is to use both. The following chapter discusses some helpful behavioral interventions, though they are less intensive than the behavioral treatments studied by the MTA.

SIDE EFFECTS AND HEALTHY ADJUSTMENTS

The dose of stimulants (or any other medications) needed to produce benefits while minimizing side effects differs among individuals. The dose almost always needs to be varied to balance the benefits and side effects, and this process usually requires a number of small adjustments. That means the doctor who prescribes the medication chooses a starting dose, measures the effect on ADHD symptoms, and then adjusts the dose, frequency, or timing of the medication for the best results.

There is often some confusion among patients about the effects and side effects of the drugs in the months after stimulant medication is prescribed, especially if the prescribing doctor is doing his or her job well and changing the prescription as needed. Possible side effects of stimulants include facial tics, like the one Jason experienced, as well as changes in moods or sleep patterns. The difficulty is that these kinds of side effects can also occur when no medication is being given and can even be part of the ADHD symptoms themselves. Also, as with Jason, one medication may cause side effects while another doesn't. So it is important to maintain contact with a doctor knowledge-able in the treatment of ADHD while treatment is continuing, especially until the best dose and medication have been deter-mined. Also, while most people don't have bad side effects from stimulants, a doctor familiar with ADHD can tell whether non-stimulant medications should be used because of stimulant side effects or if the ADHD is complicated by other problems.

Different doctors have different theories about how to start and adjust doses of ADHD medications, but one school of thought is to start with a low to moderate dose and increase it as long as the medication is not causing bad side effects, because higher doses of stimulants will generally be more helpful for the ADHD symptoms. Another school of thought is to stop increas-ing the dose as soon as it becomes effective. The best approach may depend on the individual patient's feelings about being medicated and tolerance to side effects.

STIMULANT MEDICATIONS

Stimulant medications can be divided by type of medication and by duration of delivery. There are still only two major types of stimulants commonly used for treating ADHD. The first, amphetamine, is the type of stimulant in Benzedrine. Benzedrine is not used anymore because of the side effects believed to be caused by l-amphetamine, but d-amphetamine (Dexedrine, Dextrostat) is still used to treat ADHD. The other kind of commonly used stimulant, which is more popular than amphetamine, is methylphenidate (Ritalin, Methylin, Focalin), which is similar to amphetamine in many ways.

Many of the advances in stimulant ADHD medication have come from new chemical or physical delivery systems, such as the time-release system, rather than new drugs replacing old drugs. The medications themselves are still mostly based on fast-acting amphetamines and methylphenidate, but different delivery systems have been developed to release the drug into the system over longer periods of time. Table 6.1 shows some of the brand names these drugs are sold under, broken down by drug and how long each drug is effective.

AMPHETAMINE STIMULANTS

Amphetamines have a number of effects on the brain. They cause dopamine (and other neurotransmitters, to a smaller extent) to be released into the synapses, and they compete with the real neurotransmitters for reuptake. Both of these functions cause there to be more dopamine in the synapses more of the time.

Lazar Edeleanu, a Romanian chemist, first synthesized amphetamine in 1887. The amphetamine he synthesized was the same combination of l-amphetamine and d-amphetamine later sold as Benzedrine and refined to the active d-amphetamine as Dexedrine. Amphetamines have been used for a wide variety of illnesses. One major use was as a diet aid, since they decrease appetite, though this is no longer an approved use in the United States. The major medical uses of amphetamines today are as treatment for ADHD and narcolepsy, a disorder that results in falling asleep at varying times during the day even with plenty of sleep during the night.

The full chemical name of dextroamphetamine as it is usually given in medication is dextroamphetamine sulfate, which means that the dextroamphetamine molecule is connected to another molecule called a sulfate in a kind of chemical relationship called a salt. Another ADHD drug, Adderall, has a slightly different composition. It is a mixture of four different amphetamine salts, which are intended to act at different rates and provide a more gradual decrease in the effect of the drug.

Table 6.1 Attention-Deficit/Hyperactivity Disorder Medications

TRADE NAMES	DRUG	DRUG TYPE	DOSES PER DAY	HOURS PER DOSE
Ritalin, Metadate, Methylin, others	methylphenidate	stimulant	2-3	3-5
Focalin	dextro-methylphenidate	stimulant	2-3	3-5
Ritalin SR, Metadate ER, Methylin ER	methylphenidate	stimulant	1-2	5-8
Ritalin LA, Metadate CD, Concerta	methylphenidate	stimulant	1	8+
Dexedrine, DextroStat	dextroamphetamine	stimulant	2-3	3-5
Dexedrine Spansule	dextroamphetamine	stimulant	1-2	5-8
Adderall	Mixed amphetamine salts	stimulant	1-2	5-8
Adderall XR	Mixed amphetamine salts	stimulant	1	8+
Strattera	atomoxetine	norepinephrine reuptake inhibitor	1-2	n/a
Tofranil	imipramine	antidepressant	2-3	n/a
Norpramin	desipramine	antidepressant	2-3	n/a
Wellbutrin	bupropion	antidepressant	2	n/a
Wellbutrin SR	bupropion	antidepressant	1-2	n/a
Wellbutrin XL	bupropion	antidepressant	1	n/a
Clonidine, Catapres, Catapres TTS (patch)	clonidine	blood pressure medication	2-4	n/a

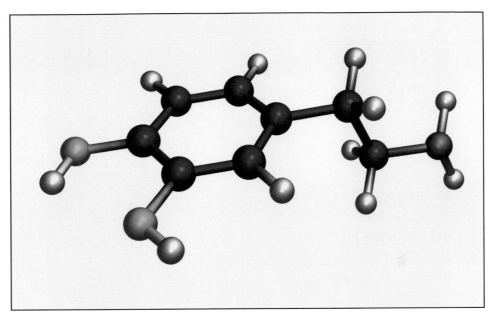

Figure 6.1 Dopamine molecule. There is strong evidence that changes in the parts of the brain related to the neurotransmitter dopamine are associated with ADHD. © *Dr Tim Evans / Photo Researchers, Inc.*

Adderall was originally marketed as a long-acting medication, but is usually given twice a day like Dexedrine, though a longer-acting form, Adderall XR, is also available.

As with methylphenidate stimulants, most longer-acting amphetamine medications are dextroamphetamine with a special delivery system that gives the same drug over a longer period of time.

METHYLPHENIDATE-BASED STIMULANTS

Methylphenidate is a dopamine reuptake inhibitor. This means that it blocks dopamine transporters, causing more dopamine to be present in the synapse.

Ciba Pharmaceutical Company, a predecessor of Novartis, patented the drug in 1954, considerably later than dextroamphetamine. Despite its later release, methylphenidate is now

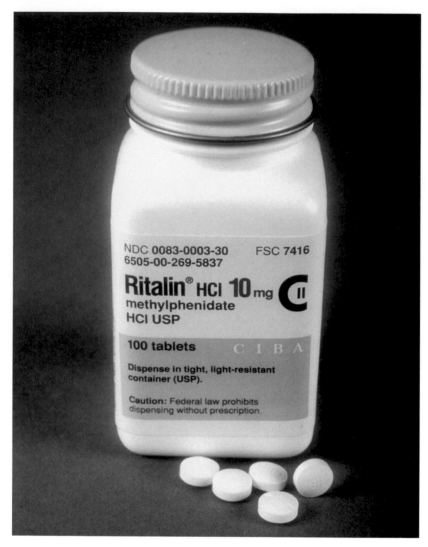

Figure 6.2 Methylphenidate is now the most commonly prescribed medication for ADHD. Ritalin is the best-known brand name version of the drug. © *Getty Images*

the most commonly prescribed medication for ADHD. The best-known brand name of methylphenidate is still Novartis's Ritalin and the extended release Ritalin SR and Ritalin SA, though the drug is also available in a number of other short-acting and extended-release brand names, including the single-dose medications Concerta and Metadate CD.

Like amphetamine, methylphenidate comes in dextro- and levo- forms. Ritalin and most methylphenidate drugs are racemic mixtures, combinations of the d- and l- forms. Focalin, like Dexedrine for amphetamines, is only made up of the d-methylphenidate form.

COMPARING STIMULANTS

Methylphenidate and amphetamine are common treatments for ADHD, but which one is better? Certainly methylphenidate is more common than amphetamine. The medications work in relatively similar ways and over relatively similar time frames. According to a recent study, the effectiveness of the two types of stimulants was similar, though methylphenidate had fewer side effects than dextroamphetamine.[25] Another study found a trend—but not a **significant** one—towards better effectiveness of methylphenidate, [26] and a companion study also found fewer side effects with methylphenidate.[27]

While there might seem to be some reasons to prefer methylphenidate, the two drugs are very similar in effectiveness, and it is likely that individual variation in which drug is more effective is more important than the small differences between drugs in a large population. Unfortunately, studies attempting to predict which stimulant medication would be best for individuals have not been very successful. Fortunately, both stimulants are very often useful for treating ADHD.

STIMULANT SIDE EFFECTS: FACT AND FICTION

Stimulant medications have been the subject of a remarkable amount of controversy, from legitimate scientific questions about the importance of side effects to objections with very little scientific basis. The side effects of stimulants are not serious for most people, but they can be. The choice to take stimulants should be made carefully with frequent input from a trusted doctor with ADHD experience.

When trying to sort fact from fiction about stimulants for ADHD, always consider the source of the information. Does a writer seem to have an agenda or something to gain? Is a particular company or group that might bias their opinions

Stimulants and the Military

Having taken stimulant medication, even properly prescribed for the treatment of ADHD, in the past year is grounds for ineligibility for military service. Of course, this is not limited to Ritalin—many prescription drugs that are commonly used for chronic disorders can bar military service.

The rules were relaxed a few years ago, probably because of the growing percentage of potential recruits who have been prescribed the drug at some point in their lives. In the past, any history of ADHD treatment barred individuals from serving in the military without a difficult-to-obtain exception. The current standard is reasonable school performance (if applicable) without medication in the previous year, and no overt signs of ADHD.

The decision to make stimulant use a criterion for denying military service is somewhat ironic. One of the first widespread uses of stimulants was during World War II, when German officer Erwin Rommel, the Desert Fox, gave them to his troops to increase their effectiveness. The Japanese, English, and Americans also gave stimulants to their troops. In fact, the U.S. Air Force gives amphetamines (Dexedrine) ("go-pills") to pilots to help them manage fatigue during a mission.

supporting the writer? (This book should not be an exception to this rule. The author has no affiliation with or financial interest in any group that makes ADHD medications, nor with any group opposing stimulant medication.) It is a good idea to consult multiple sources and seek opinions from more than one expert or professional.

STIMULANT MEDICATION AND HEART PROBLEMS

The FDA recently decided not to put "black box" warnings on stimulants, reversing a split decision (8 to 7) of an advisory panel, a group of experts who recommend courses of action to the agency, to do so. A black box warning is a strong statement of risk with bolded text inside a highly visible black rectangle. A reversal like this is unusual for the FDA, highlighting how controversial the question of a relationship between stimulants and heart problems has become.

Increases in blood pressure and pulse rate after short- and long-term stimulant treatment seem to be common, though the increases observed were often not statistically significant or clinically important in otherwise healthy children and adults.[28] Adults with high blood pressure are probably most at risk, and should certainly be monitored.[29] Interestingly, the study found that some nonstimulant medications for ADHD, bupropion and desipramine, also raised blood pressure.

The close relationship between the structure of the illegal drug methamphetamine, which is known to cause heart problems, and the ADHD drugs dextroamphetamine and methylphenidate, coupled with documentation of a rise in blood pressure from stimulant medications, made the panel look carefully at the possibility of a problem. There have also been reports of sudden unexpected deaths (SUD) in patients taking stimulants as directed, though many of these were in adult patients and many are thought to have happened in patients with heart problems that had not been recognized before they started taking stimulants.

This controversy is likely to continue as the FDA and doctors try to find a balance between increasing awareness of stimulants' potential to worsen heart problems and not scaring away patients who could benefit from the effects of stimulants on ADHD.

STIMULANTS AND HEIGHT

Another area of controversy over the years has been whether low-dose stimulants slow or reduce growth. While this topic is still controversial, a follow-up to the MTA study is the largest study of the question so far, with weight and height measurements for 433 individuals.[30] It found that there was a significant but small effect of stimulants on growth, at least in the first 14 months of the study. After 14 months, the group assigned to behavior therapy had grown 6.19 centimeters (about 2.4 inches) and the group assigned to a carefully crafted dose of stimulant medication, which is higher than the lowest effective dose often given, had grown 4.75 cm (about 1.9 inches). The stimulant medication seemed to have lowered growth by 1.44 cm (just over half an inch) over 14 months. In the 10 months following, however, there was no significant difference in growth. This is consistent with later studies that found no long-term difference in growth[31] and a similar initial decrease in growth rate followed by a trend back toward normal growth.[32] While it is not formally known whether stimulants affect final adult height, it is likely that the effect, if any, is small.

STIMULANT MEDICATION AND LONG-TERM
LEARNING/ACADEMIC ACHIEVEMENT

Stimulants certainly make it more possible for people with ADHD to demonstrate what they have learned. They make it possible to complete homework assignments, take tests, and answer questions without becoming distracted. They also make it possible to pay attention to class work by increasing focus and decreasing disruptive behavior. These short-term effects are obvious and have been described many times. Some studies have examined the effects of stimulants on grades shortly after starting stimulant treatment, and these studies are generally positive, as expected. One study looked at the quantity and accuracy of math and reading problems attempted on stimulants and found that both were improved, at least over the 11 weeks the research lasted.[33]

It is less clear whether stimulants have an effect on how well academic or other information is learned over a long period of time. One part of the problem is deciding on a good control group for a long-term study. Ideally, some of the people in the study would receive stimulants and some would receive only ineffective placebos, and nobody would know who received what until the study was over. This is known as a double-blind trial, but it is hard to conduct such a trial over a long period of time. Another part of the problem is carefully deciding what learning and academic achievement mean. Do they mean standardized tests, grades, or some broader measure of how well the person receiving treatment gets on in a school environment?

The MTA study, using standardized tests, showed no significant improvement in academic achievement as defined by a standardized test of skills with stimulant treatments, with the exception of combined behavior and medication treatment, which was somewhat better than treatment by behavior alone for a standard test of reading ability. Of course, standardized tests measure a complicated mixture of intelligence and recall, and stimulant medications certainly do not change intelligence. They probably do not greatly affect long-term recall either, so it is not very surprising that they have little effect on standardized tests.

If academic achievement is measured by grades, it is at least likely that some improvement during long-term stimulant treatment will be seen, though literature on this point is surprisingly thin and studies do not tend to be much longer than a year.[34] Conservatively, there is not enough information to answer the question of how much effect stimulant medications has on grades. Anecdotally, the effects of stimulants on the effectiveness of tutoring seem to be positive, at least for people with severe ADHD, because it helps to increase attention and attention span enough that more of the session can be dedicated to teaching concepts and ideas and less to keeping the person's attention.

NONSTIMULANT MEDICATIONS

Nonstimulant medications used to treat ADHD include several antidepressants and a blood pressure medication. In most cases, the mechanism by which these medications work is less well understood than for stimulants. These medications can affect ADHD symptoms, but they often have more side effects and take longer to work. Unlike a stimulant, which can have an effect in minutes, these medications, which include atomoxetine, bupropion, the tricyclic antidepressants, and clonidine, may require up to three weeks before their effects can be seen. This is because they probably work by modifying the number and kind of molecules (receptors and transporters) on the surface of the synapses, which can take time to accomplish.

Recently, Strattera and other antidepressants have been associated with an increase in suicidal thoughts in children in a small fraction of patients, generally near the beginning of treatment. While the overall rate of actual suicides was similar with and without drug treatment, it is a side effect that has been frequently discussed in the press and is worth considering when starting treatment with these drugs.

Strattera (atomoxetine). Most nonstimulant medications for ADHD are commonly used for other purposes, such as anti-depressants and blood pressure medications. Atomoxetine is primarily an ADHD medication. It is a norepinephrine reup-take inhibitor, which means that it makes norepinephrine more available by preventing it from being taken out of the synapse. This mechanism is similar to that of stimulants that make more dopamine available and certain types of antidepressants that make serotonin more available. As discussed in Chapter 3, making dopamine and norepinephrine more available can help ADHD symptoms. Strattera has been associated with rare liver complications, and liver problems should be carefully watched for while taking the drug.

Wellbutrin (bupropion). Bupropion is an antidepressant, but its chemical structure and effects are quite different from other antidepressants, including the tricyclic antidepressants, which are also used to treat ADHD. Bupropion inhibits uptake of norepinephrine and dopamine and probably has an effect on ADHD as a result. Bupropion side effects can include seizure, and Wellbutrin should be avoided in anyone who is prone to seizures.

Tricyclic antidepressants (TCAs). Tricyclic antidepressants are drugs that were commonly used to treat depression before drugs like Prozac and Paxil, often known as selective serotonin reuptake inhibitors (SSRIs), became available. Tricyclic anti-depressants such as Norpramin (desipramine) and Tofranil (imipramine) are still used to treat depression when SSRIs don't work and are a second-line treatment for ADHD. They are par-ticularly useful when tics and other side effects from stimulants are bothersome. They last longer but have more side effects than stimulants. They also can have the effect of lowering heart rate

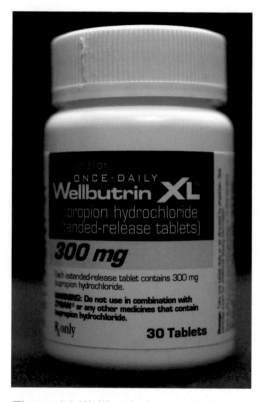

Figure 6.3 Wellbutrin (bupropion), a nonstimulant medication used to treat ADHD, inhibits uptake of norepinephrine and dopamine. © *Getty Images*

and require electrocardiograms (a way of measuring heart activity) and regular blood tests (to check levels of the medication), so they are much less convenient than stimulants.

Clonidine. Clonidine is used to treat high blood pressure (hypertension) but can also produce changes in mood and behavior that can help people with ADHD who do not respond to stimulants. While it is not as useful as stimulants at increasing attention, it can help decrease hyperactivity and impulsiveness and increase cooperativeness, which can be particularly useful when ADHD and oppositional defiant disorders are both present. Since clonidine is a blood pressure medication, it can have effects on blood pressure and the heart and, like the tricyclic antidepressants, requires considerable monitoring.

THE PLACEBO EFFECT . . . ON OTHER PEOPLE!

When ADHD medication, especially stimulant medication, works well, it changes the individual a lot in a very short time. It brings them new resources and ability to focus and pay attention to work. Medication is a valuable tool for rapidly dealing with ADHD symptoms, but it can change the way people perceive the individual in good and bad ways. This depends on who knows the person with ADHD is taking medication and their beliefs about medication for ADHD. If the reaction is positive, the perceived changes may also be positive. With ADHD, given the remarkable changes in behavior that actually can happen in a short time with stimulant medications, this is the more common experience, at least for interactions with parents and teachers. Parents and teachers who expect that a child will be less hyperactive and more attentive will often believe that the child's behavior has changed much more than it actually has.

Just In: Time Release

Stimulant medications are all fast acting. The instant release (IR) versions dissolve quickly and have an effect only for a few hours. Longer-acting stimulant medications are the same drugs, but clever engineering of the pills allows them to release the stimulant over time. One of the simplest ways to engineer a long acting dose is used for Dexedrine Spansules, which are small beads of medication inside a capsule that dissolve at different rates, delivering the dose over a longer period. Ritalin LA is similar, with two sets of beads, one of which dissolves quickly, while the other dissolves several hours later. Concerta uses an entirely different system, called OROS. This system uses a capsule that doesn't dissolve, coated with methylphenidate. The methylphenidate coating dissolves quickly, and water slowly enters the capsule, wetting a piece of spongelike material called an expander. The expander pushes the methylphenidate inside the capsule out slowly through a hole, releasing the drug.

Of course, the other side of this external placebo effect also occurs. If a person thinks of medication as a sign of weakness or that something is "just wrong" with the person taking the medication, they may not react positively regardless of the actual effect of the medication. Education is really the only antidote for this negative effect. The more people learn about ADHD, the more positively they tend to react to learning about the disorder in those around them.

Living with ADHD: Changing the Inside and Outside Worlds

Anyone reading this chapter for advice on their own ADHD will probably want it to be short and to the point. Here it is.

Three Steps for Getting Things Done!

1. Break things into bite-sized bits (and write the bits down in lists).
2. Make structural (specific, concrete, and repeated) plans for getting the lists done.
3. Take advantage of (and ask for) help to make plans, and make plans happen.

Breaking Things into Bite-Sized Bits. One of the most important things for people with ADHD to do is to take things in small steps. Instead of making time for "doing homework," for instance, it helps to break homework down into math, science, English, social studies, or other specific subjects. Lists help a lot in breaking things down. Getting into the habit of writing homework, chores, or other tasks down as they are assigned and reinforcing that habit whenever possible can help. It's even good advice for people without ADHD.

Making Structural Plans for Getting Things Done. Lists are a good start, but they're not much use without plans for turning the lists into accomplishments. For people with ADHD, structure is an even more important part of getting things done than it is for most people. For homework, this might mean having a particular time, place, and plan for doing the work.

Taking Advantage of Help to Make Plans and Make Plans Happen. If you have ADHD, it can be hard to remember to do something long enough to make it a habit and hard to keep up with the habit when you do remember. Having other people to help you remember and to keep you on task can help with this.

For people still living at home, parents are often an important resource. They can help break assignments and tasks into small pieces, help make good plans for getting the pieces done, and help provide supportive nudges. Teachers can help too, both by providing order in the classroom and by making sure that things like homework assignments are written down before a student leaves the classroom. Help can also come from a number of sources, including family, friends, and professionals. For example, Don, whose ADHD has lasted into adulthood, has a longtime friend who drops by once a month to help him organize his checkbook and make sure bills are paid. It takes about half an hour and then they go out for dinner. Don buys—it's a heck of a lot cheaper than all the late fees he used to get.

A BREAK, MAKE, AND TAKE EXAMPLE

For Jason, mentioned in Chapter 6, homework had become quite a frustration. His tutor advised him to break it down as much as possible. He gave him a small notepad with his class schedule already printed on it and asked him to make sure his assignments or "none" were written in each period before he left the classroom. For students with more severe ADHD, a teacher can help make sure this is done. When Jason forgot something, the first thing he did in his tutoring session was call a classmate and get the assignment, which also worked well. If the teacher mentioned an upcoming test or paper deadline, Jason was to write that down as well.

During an intensive initial period, Jason's tutor worked with him four days a week and helped him and his parents form the following plan: Jason got home from school around 4:00 P.M. He took his short-acting ADHD medication (Dexedrine) and then had free time for half an hour to give it time to take effect and give him a chance to relax from school before starting his homework. Jason always did his homework in the dining room, which had a good-sized table, could be closed off, and was quiet from 4:30 to 7:00, which usually gave him plenty of time to finish his assignments.

Jason worked with his tutor to establish a pattern for his homework. The first step was prioritizing. After Jason caught up on late work, he started daily homework with the subjects he found most challenging and rotated through the others, spending enough time (usually not more than half an hour) to finish an average assignment. If Jason got seriously stuck on something, he could move on to another assignment or a different part of the same assignment. If there was time, he came back to these parts, but at first keeping Jason's frustration level down was important. If there was time left over, he would work on longer-term projects for up to an hour—enough to make substantial progress but not so much that Jason felt burnt out. Also, before finishing, Jason and his tutor would go over to a large whiteboard calendar and write down upcoming events and assignments from Jason's pad. They also used a whiteboard to break down complicated, long assignments into simpler parts so Jason could have the satisfaction of crossing things off and making progress on larger ventures.

The dining room was a good choice of place for Jason to do his homework because it was convenient for his mother or father to stop in from the kitchen every 10 to 15 minutes and help keep him on track. Blocking off a period of time and particular space for homework is all well and good, but help staying on task can be even more important. Jason's parents were great, though, and also helped him remember to put long-term assignments on the whiteboard and to remember the other parts of the productive pattern.

CONTINUING GOOD PATTERNS + CONTINUING HELP = CONTINUING SUCCESS

Jason broke down daily assignments into subjects, broke down long assignments into simpler tasks, and broke down the time he spent on long assignments into manageable pieces. He made and kept specific, concrete, and repeated plans for approaching homework. He also took advantage of the help from his tutor, from his parents, and from his ADHD medications to make sure lists were made, plans for doing homework were kept, his attention stayed focused while working on homework, and deadlines and other important bits of information weren't lost in the daily confusion.

On a simpler level these ideas also helped with Jason's chores and responsibilities around the house. Months later, when he was again doing well in school, Jason asked his parents for a whiteboard for his room and started using the calendar on the whiteboard to remind himself of plans with friends!

PERSONALIZING FOR SUCCESS

These kinds of structures don't work for everyone. People with ADHD are unique, both in the way their ADHD expresses itself as well as in all the other ways that people differ from each other. The challenge, as with ADHD medication, is to keep trying until something works well, because something almost always does. One of the major lessons of the large ADHD treatments study (MTA) described earlier was that intensive behavioral treatment tailored to the needs of the individual, with frequent feedback and lots of involvement of the person with ADHD and their caregivers, was quite effective in treating ADHD.

The Further Resources section at the end of this book lists some wonderful books on taking advantage of the good things about ADHD and coping with the more frustrating parts of it. One excellent choice is *Taking Charge of ADHD* by ADHD researcher Russell Barkley. This book includes an excellent chapter on behavioral therapy and parenting a child with ADHD.

ADHD and Music

Not much has been published in peer-reviewed literature on the influence of music on ADHD. Studying the effects of music therapy on ADHD is somewhat difficult because it is not usually a primary or sole treatment, though music therapists generally see the outcomes as positive.[35] One study tested 20 children with ADHD and 20 without ADHD on age-appropriate arithmetic questions in environments with three different noise levels: silence, voice, and music.[36] They found that children without ADHD performed similarly in each case, while people with ADHD did somewhat better with music than with voice or silence as a background, but only when the situation with music was tested first. This is an interesting result but the study was fairly small so should be viewed with caution. Something that have an effect in a small study can sometimes have no effect in a second, larger study.

From a purely anecdotal point of view, however, improvements in concentration have been noticed in some students with ADHD when music is playing in the background, preferably energetic music without a lot lyrics and in a favorite style of the listener.

ADHD ON THE INSIDE AND OUTSIDE

Attention-deficit/hyperactivity disorder is a complicated condition, and planning how to treat ADHD is also complicated. Treatment plans should include changing the world inside (one's behavior and state of mind) and the world outside (one's surroundings, such as at home or school) to work with, not against, the strengths of the person with ADHD. Medication can be an important part of this plan, but so are changes in behavior (the inside world) and creating an environment that helps solidify those changes (the outside world).

Tutors, parents, and other caretakers working with people with ADHD over a wide range of ages must be sure to pay attention to both the inner and outer world. Sometimes it helps a great deal to bring in someone from the outside, because it's often hard to see how a familiar environment affects the way you behave, focus, and work. This is true for everyone but is even more important for people with ADHD than for most people. Forgetting to do things, starting but not finishing things, and in general "blowing off" people and responsibilities are all characteristics of ADHD, but they are also characteristics that people judge harshly. Someone from the outside with an understanding of ADHD can bring a new perspective without resentment or frustration about the past.

Many professionals can help improve the experience of living with ADHD and the effectiveness of people with ADHD in dealing with the outside world. Plenty of books and other resources also give great advice on this topic.

BUILDING UP STRUCTURE

People with ADHD, and especially with hyperactive/impulsive ADHD, often dislike structure. This may be partly because when they are expected to keep up their end of complicated obligations, it often feels overwhelming and impossible. This kind of **negative reinforcement** is a powerful influence. Unstructured environments are often less effective for people with ADHD, however, because they allow distractions and make it harder to focus effectively on one task at a time. This is especially true of learning environments. Structured learning environments with set routines and frequent contact between student and instructor are most conducive to learning for most people with ADHD, according to teachers.[37] The same study reported that preferential seating (usually putting students with ADHD near the front), short opportunities to briefly stretch or exercise called **motor breaks**, and teaching students with ADHD to self-monitor behaviors were also seen as effective. All of these are important aspects of a structured environment, internal and external, that is helpful for students with ADHD.

SELF-ESTEEM

We all need **positive reinforcement** in our lives to help us build healthy self-esteem. People with ADHD can find it difficult to get positive reinforcement because ADHD can make it harder to keep up with relationships and to accomplish goals, which are two common sources of self-esteem. It is important for people with ADHD to surround themselves with supportive people, including friends, family, and helpful professionals. All have important, but different, roles in helping to build and keep self-esteem. Another excellent way to get positive reinforcement is to succeed at getting things done, which is why lists that break goals down into simple steps can be helpful. It can be satisfying to cross even little things off a list, and that extra bit of positive reinforcement may help to keep someone with ADHD interested enough to move to the next item.

ADHD AND THE CHANGING ENVIRONMENT

Symptoms of ADHD may change in different environments. Changes in environment and expectations may help with ADHD. Consistent and adequate psychological therapy can help as well. Behavior therapy is a set of techniques that can help children with ADHD develop better reactions and habits.

Thoughts on My Son

By Jessica McCabe

My son is known to be a pencil tapper, a foot jiggler, and a tongue clucker. In response, we have provided him with an Egyptian hand drum.

My son has always loved all things military, all things projectile, all things strategic. In response, we have encouraged his interest in war history and taught him to play chess.

My son has always been distracted by colors, obsessed with things being even, driven to *pick*, *pick*, *pick* at less-than-perfect surfaces. In response, we have hosted regular craft parties and allowed him to express himself through clothing.

My son is overly dramatic, quick to tears, his own worst critic. In response, we take advantage of this time while he still wants to hug his parents, still wants a kiss to make it better.

My son struggles with learning issues, with his strong opinions, with his tendency to let his mind wander. In response, we have home schooled him since he was four years old. My son was the baby we hoped for, is the child he is supposed to be, will be the man he wants to be. Not perfect, but beautifully human.

(Reprinted with permission from a post by Jessica McCabe on an online discussion list for parents of children with ADHD.)

Some of these techniques are similarly designed to improve reactions and habits. These approaches do help, as does medication. Since ADHD is a complex disorder, it is not at all surprising that it may take a fairly complex set of approaches to effectively treat it.

8 The Outlook for ADHD

The appointment was for 10:30 a.m. on March 8, 2107, and it was already 10:28. JaredX barely had time to park his Mercedes Hover Mark VII in the doctor's vertical carport. He was late for his appointment again, which was most of the problem, really. His nanobots were acting up. That wasn't unreasonable given that they hadn't been adjusted since they took up residence in his brain when he was seven years old, but the microdoses of chemicals they created and secreted to balance JaredX's ADHD were clearly getting a little unbalanced. Lucky for JaredX, all his doctor needed to do was contact the nanobots and tell them where and when to step up production. An hour later (50 minutes in the waiting room and 10 adjusting the nanobots), JaredX was on his way.

At least it wasn't like the old days when you might have to take a pill once a week to adjust your ADHD. "Still, what a nuisance," JaredX thought. If he had been born a few years later, the nanobots would have been 802.11wk compatible and the doctor could have contacted them via the Internet and made the adjustment online.

NEW INSIGHTS, NEW TREATMENTS

For a disorder that has been identified for more than a hundred years, ADHD is the topic of a remarkable amount of ongoing investigation. As of March 8, 2007, 100 years before JaredX had his nanobots adjusted, there were 15,682 articles on "attention deficit" in the Medline database of scientific literature, and such a simple attempt at searching is likely to miss many older articles that use different terms for the disorder.

As scientists' sophistication in understanding the neurobiology and genetics of ADHD grows, they will be able to develop new kinds of drugs and treatments. They might even be able to develop drugs that will protect against prenatal changes that make ADHD more likely. Even further in the future they may be able to create smart medicines that deliver themselves to exactly where they are needed using **nanotechnology**. It is science fiction now, but JaredX's nanobots could become reality someday.

As tools, methods, and outlooks change, so do the questions that need to be asked about ADHD. The past decade has seen incredible advances in biological techniques, especially developments in studies of the **genome**, genetic studies, understanding the brain in humans and in animal models, and the development of new treatment ideas and options. The studies of ADHD that these techniques make possible are just beginning.

NEW GENETIC STUDIES

While several genes have been strongly linked to ADHD, there are more genes that may be linked to the disorder. In the past it has been necessary to have a solid hypothesis about which gene or genes were involved. After making an educated guess, data collection and carefully examining the association of one or a few genes with ADHD could take several years. Clearly this was not a very fast method given the 30,000 or more genes in the human genome. Another possibility, described earlier, is linkage analysis among related families, but this too is a relatively slow way of finding connections between genetics and ADHD.

Fortunately, over the course of the next 10 to 20 years, scientists should be able to figure out most of the genes that affect the group of traits we call ADHD. As technology has changed,

Using the Internet for Researching ADHD

The Internet has an amazing amount of information on every topic imaginable, and certainly has plenty of material on ADHD. Unfortunately, the quality of information on the Internet is extremely variable. In the Further Resources section at the end of this book, there is a list of Web sites with reputable and informative content. Most of the information in these pages is likely to represent the current thinking on ADHD. Even on these trusted sites, the quality of information will vary, and as is the case with a book or any other source, just because it's written down doesn't mean it's true. Use caution and good judgment when using the Internet to research ADHD.

A good way to decide how much to trust a site is to look at what is called its top-level domain, the letters or the Web address after the last period. This tells you a little bit about who made and runs the site. If the site is run by the U.S. government, the Web address ends in *.gov*, and the site has probably been read over many times by scientists interested in its accuracy, a process called peer review. Government-run sites with useful information on ADHD include http://www.cdc.gov/ncbddd/adhd, the Centers for Disease Control and Prevention (CDC) home page on ADHD.

Sites ending in *.org* belong to nonprofit organizations such as http://www.chadd.org and http://www.add.org with an interest in ADHD. Unlike *.gov* sites, these sites present information that may not have been subject to peer review and should be considered carefully. Not all organizations interested in ADHD provide complete, up-to-date, or accurate information on the disorder.

Sites whose Web address ends in *.edu* can be a great resource. These are Web pages associated with educational institutions and are often maintained by researchers who study ADHD professionally.

The last main type of commonly seen site is the familiar *.com*. These are commercial sites, and as always be cautious about information found on sites trying to sell something. That said, http://www.adhd.com, a site about ADHD sponsored by Eli Lilly (Strattera), and http://www.focusonadhd.com, a site sponsored by McNeil Laboratories (Concerta), provide quite a bit of accurate and detailed ADHD information, so *.com* sites are not automatically bad.

These Web sites, like popular books on ADHD (including this one), are considered "secondary literature." In other words, someone has read reports written by scientists who study ADHD and interpreted them for the reader in an easier to understand format. It used to be the case that the reports themselves, the "primary literature," or "medical literature" were available only in special libraries, usually located at colleges and universities.

Because there was no easy way to search the literature, the only way to become familiar with it was to go to one of these libraries and spend many hours reading through papers in search of information. Later, by the late 1980s, electronic search services were available, though it used to cost $20 or more for each simple search. (Imagine spending $20 for a Google search.) Now you can do much more powerful searches of the primary literature for free. The National Library of Medicine (http://www.nlm.gov) offers access to MEDLINE, a vast collection of abstracts and references covering almost all of the important medical literature of the past half-century.

it has become possible to do larger, more effective studies that can examine association between many genes at once. It would be easy to think that this would be the end of ADHD research, but really it will raise even more questions than it solves—new questions that could not be asked before. (This is a common pattern in research. New information seldom ends inquiries. Instead it opens the door for new questions.)

GENETIC TESTS AND THE CHALLENGE OF GENE THERAPY

After all the genes that influence ADHD are identified, scientists can ask new questions. One of the first is whether it is possible to predict who is most likely to develop ADHD. If this prediction can be made reasonably accurately, quantitative genetic tests can be developed. Since the majority of the components that affect ADHD happen during development, this test might be commonly given to embryos fairly early in development. As a prenatal test, it could help identify embryos that might benefit from more or different care of their prenatal environment. For instance, since smoking while pregnant is a risk factor for ADHD, if an embryo has a genetic profile that indicates a high risk for ADHD, it might be even more important for the birth mother to avoid smoking during pregnancy.

As a postnatal (after birth) test given to young children, such a test could help psychiatrists determine whether the difficulties a particular child is experiencing are more or less likely to be due to ADHD. More importantly, it might help to determine which treatments are likely to be best for which child. Remember that although stimulants are remarkably effective for a large fraction of the people with ADHD, there is still no way to know whether stimulants will be effective for a given person, and no way to know which stimulant or dosage would be best when stimulants are effective. Understanding these questions will allow much more personalized, specific, and effective medication of ADHD, with fewer side effects. The value of this making these kinds of decisions based on genetic information is called **personalized medicine.** It will also allow doctors to understand who is most likely to benefit from the wide variety of behavioral techniques for helping children (and parents) cope with ADHD.

Understanding which genes affect the symptoms of a particular person with ADHD may help explain the reasons each person's symptoms develop as they do. This kind of understanding may help doctors break ADHD into many different disorders that have a similar set of symptoms. The more specific they can be about what is causing a particular person's ADHD, the better equipped they will be to treat their symptoms.

Another promising area for understanding ADHD is **gene therapy.** Gene therapy harnesses the power of genetics to replace or supplement genes that increase the likelihood that a person will suffer from ADHD with better copies of those same genes. For a disorder such as ADHD that seems to develop at least partly from changes that happen before birth, gene therapy would probably be most useful very early.

OLD DRUGS GIVEN NEW LIFE

In addition to developing new drugs, scientists may also be able to revisit the many old drugs that were not approved because of rare side effects. One example would be modafinil (Provigil), which was shown to be effective for treating ADHD but is not approved for that purpose because of concerns over Stevens-Johnson syndrome, a rare but potentially deadly allergic reaction of the skin that usually results from a bad reaction to a drug. If doctors could predict accurately who would get the side effect, they could use modafinil for ADHD and simply make sure not to give it to people who are likely to get Stevens-Johnson syndrome.

LONG-TERM STUDIES OF TREATMENT

While stimulants have been available and in common use for some time, the ideas of adult ADHD and continuing stimulant treatment over a lifetime are relatively new, as are the nonstimulant treatments for ADHD. Most studies of ADHD treatments have lasted only a few years, though there is also some research looking at the lifetime effects of stimulant treatment.

Such treatment studies are hard to fund, since they last far longer than the typical three- to five-year funding period for grants from the National Institutes of Health, the major source of money for studying ADHD and other disorders that affect human health. Long-term studies are also hard to conduct because they require a researcher who is interested in studying ADHD over a long period of time and able to track the same patient population for many years.

SHIFTING THOUGHTS ON THE ENDS OF THE SPECTRUM

Another challenge to understanding of ADHD is the social debate surrounding the disorder. There is a popular perception of an epidemic of ADHD diagnosis and a great deal of debate about whether this represents better diagnosis of ADHD, too much diagnosis of ADHD, or an increase in the number of people with ADHD. Attention-deficit/hyperactivity disorder and many similar disorders are characterized by extremes on the spectrum of behavior rather than by clearly separate categories of "abnormal" versus "normal" behavior. As these kinds of disorders become better understood, it is becoming clear that many apparent "moral" or "disciplinary" disorders have real biological basis. Society generally excuses behaviors with a biological basis and disciplines behaviors with no biological basis, so this shift in understanding challenges social responses.

Human beings vary in many ways. It's important to value this amazing variety. When these variations make life difficult, it is good for society to research ways to lessen those difficulties, but it must be remembered that variation itself is important and valuable. It is crucially important that any definition of ADHD as a *disorder*, rather than simply a set of traits, continues to require interference with a person's ability to function in their life. This is the most difficult thing about disorders that fall along a spectrum. The same traits that may require medication or other interventions in one person may not require any action in another. One of the most difficult parts of treating ADHD and similar disorders in the future may be figuring out where variation becomes disorder. This is a difficult question, and one that, even as our tools for understanding and treating ADHD improve by leaps and bounds, will be best answered as it is today: one person at a time.

NOTES

1. S.P. Cuffe, C.G. Moore, and R.E. McKeown, "Prevalence and Correlates of ADHD Symptoms in the National Health Interview Survey," *Journal of Attention Disorders* 9, no. 2 (2005): 392–401.

2. B.B. Lahey et al., "Instability of the DSM-IV Subtypes of ADHD from Preschool through Elementary School," *Archives of General Psychiatry* 62, no. 8 (2005): 896–902.

3. Ibid.

4. A. Diamond, "Attention-Deficit Disorder (Attention-Deficit/ Hyperactivity Disorder Without Hyperactivity): A Neurobiologically and Behaviorally Distinct Disorder from Attention-Deficit/Hyperactivity Disorder (With Hyperactivity)," *Developmental Psychopathology* 17, no. 3 (2005): 807–825.

5. R.J. Neuman, et al., "Latent Class Analysis of ADHD and Comorbid Symptoms in a Population Sample of Adolescent Female Twins," *Journal of Child Psychology and Psychiatry* 42, no. 7 (2001): 933–42.

6. P.H. Wender, *Attention-Deficit Hyperactivity Disorder in Adults* (New York: Oxford University Press, 1995).

7. J.J. McGough and R.A. Barkley, "Diagnostic Controversies in Adult Attention Deficit Hyperactivity Disorder," *American Journal of Psychiatry* 161, no. 11 (2004): 1948–1956.

8. R.A. Barkley, *Taking Charge of ADHD: The Complete, Authoritative Guide for Parents* (New York: The Guilford Press, 2005).

9. F.X. Castellanos, et al., "Developmental Trajectories of Brain Volume Abnormalities in Children and Adolescents with Attention-Deficit/ Hyperactivity Disorder," *Journal of the American Medical Association* 288, no. 14 (2002): 1740–1748.

10. R. DeLong, "Medical and Pharmacologic Treatment of Learning Disabilities," *Journal of Child Neurology* 10, Suppl. 1 (1995): S92–S95.

11. C.R. Mahoney, et al., "Effect of Breakfast Composition on Cognitive Processes in Elementary School Children," *Physiology and Behavior* 85, no. 5 (2005): 635–645.

12. M. Kinsbourne, "Sugar and the Hyperactive Child," *New England Journal of Medicine* 330, no. 5 (1994): 355–356.

13. R.J. Prinz, W.A. Roberts, and E. Hantman, "Dietary Correlates of Hyperactive Behavior in Children," *Journal of Consulting Clinical Psychology* 48, no. 6 (1980): 760–769.

14. M.L. Wolraich, et al., "Effects of Diets High in Sucrose or Aspartame on the Behavior and Cognitive Performance of Children," *New England Journal of Medicine* 330, no. 5 (1994): 301–307.

15. N.M. Avena and B.G. Hoebel, "A Diet Promoting Sugar Dependency Causes Behavioral Cross-Sensitization to a Low Dose of Amphetamine," *Neuroscience* 122, no. 1 (2003): 17–20.

16. K.A. Kavale and S.R. Forness, "Hyperactivity and Diet Treatment: A Meta-Analysis of the Feingold Hypothesis," *Journal of Learning Disabilities* 16, no. 6 (1983): 324–330.

17. J. Egger, et al., "Controlled Trial of Oligoantigenic Treatment in the Hyperkinetic Syndrome," *Lancet* 1, no. 8428 (1985): 540-545; I. Pollock and J.O. Warner, "Effect of Artificial Food Colours on Childhood Behaviour," *Archives of Disease in Childhood* 65, no. 1 (1990): 74–77.

18. N. Roth, et al., "Coincidence of Attention Deficit Disorder and Atopic Disorders in Children: Empirical Findings and Hypothetical Background," *Journal of Abnormal Childhood Psychology* 19, no. 1 (1991): 1–13.

19. A. Brawley, et al., "Allergic Rhinitis in Children with Attention-Deficit/Hyperactivity Disorder," *Annals of Allergy Asthma and Immunology* 92, no. 6 (2004): 663–667.

20. L.E. Arnold, et al., "Serum Zinc Correlates with Parent- and Teacher-Rated Inattention in Children with Attention-Deficit/Hyperactivity Disorder," *Journal of Childhood and Adolescent Psychopharmacology* 15, no. 4 (2005): 628–636.

21. L.E. Arnold, et al., "Megavitamins for Minimal Brain Dysfunction. A placebo-controlled study," *Journal of the American Medical Association* 240, no. 24 (1978): 2642–2643.

22. R.H. Haslam, J.T. Dalby, and A.W. Rademaker, "Effects of Megavitamin Therapy on Children with Attention Deficit Disorders," *Pediatrics* 74, no. 1 (1984): 103–111.

23. D.A. Christakis et al., "Early Television Exposure and Subsequent Attentional Problems in Children." *Pediatrics* 113, no. 4 (2004): 708–713.

24. Rupert Mellor, "Interview: Jack Be Nimble, Jack Be Quick," *The Times*, September 17, 2005.

25. W.J. Barbaresi, et al., "Long-Term Stimulant Medication Treatment of Attention-Deficit/Hyperactivity Disorder: Results from a Population-Based Study," *Journal of Developmental and Behavioral Pediatrics* 27, no 1 (2006): 1–10.

26. D. Efron, F. Jarman, and M. Barker, "Methylphenidate versus Dexamphetamine in Children with Attention Deficit Hyperactivity Disorder: A Double-Blind, Crossover Trial," *Pediatrics* 100, no 6 (1997): E6.

27. D. Efron, F. Jarman, and M. Barker, "Side Effects of Methylphenidate and Dexamphetamine in Children with Attention Deficit Hyperactivity Disorder: A Double-Blind, Crossover Trial," *Pediatrics* 100, no. 4 (1997): 662–666.

28. R.L. Findling, et al., "Short- and Long-Term Cardiovascular Effects of Mixed Amphetamine Salts Extended Release in Children," *Journal of Pediatrics* 147, no. 3 (2005):348–54; R.H. Weisler, J. Biederman, T.J. Spencer, and T.E. Wilens, "Long-Term Cardiovascular Effects of Mixed Amphetamine Salts Extended Release in Adults with ADHD," *CNS Spectrums* 10 (12 Suppl 20) (2005): 35–43.

29. T.E. Wilens, P.G. Hammerness, J. Biederman, A. Kwon, T.J. Spencer, S. Clark, M. Scott, A. Podolski, J.W. Ditterline, M.C. Morris, and

H. Moore, "Blood Pressure Changes Associated with Medication Treatment of Adults with Attention-Deficit/Hyperactivity Disorder," *Journal of Clinical Psychiatry* 66, no. 2 (2005): 253–259.

30. MTA Cooperative Group, "National Institute of Mental Health Multimodal Treatment Study of ADHD Follow-Up: Changes in Effectiveness and Growth After the End of Treatment," *Pediatrics* 113, no. 4 (2004): 762–769.

31. D.A. Zachor, A.W. Roberts, J.B. Hodgens, J.S. Isaacs, and J. Merrick, "Effects of Long-Term Psychostimulant Medication on Growth of Children with ADHD," *Research in Developmental Disabilities* 27, no 2 (2006): 162–174.

32. S.V. Faraone, J. Biederman, M. Monuteaux, and T. Spencer, "Long-Term Effects of Extended-Release Mixed Amphetamine Salts Treatment of Attention-Deficit/Hyperactivity Disorder on Growth," *Journal of Childhood and Adolescent Psychopharmacology* 15, no. 2 (2005): 191–202.

33. J. Elia, P.A. Welsh, C.S. Gullotta, and J.L. Rapoport, "Classroom Academic Performance: Improvement with both Methylphenidate and Dextroamphetamine in ADHD Boys," *Journal of Childhood Psychology and Psychiatry* 34, no. 5 (1993): 785–804.

34. R. Schachar, et al., "Attention-Deficit Hyperactivity Disorder: Critical Appraisal of Extended Treatment Studies," *Canadian Journal of Psychiatry* 47, no. 4 (2002): 337–348.

35. N.A. Jackson. "A Survey of Music Therapy Methods and Their Role in the Treatment of Early Elementary School Children with ADHD," *Journal of Music Therapy* 40, no. 4 (2003): 302–323.

36. H. Abikoff, M.E. Courtney, P.J. Szeibel, and H.S. Koplewicz, "The Effects of Auditory Stimulation on the Arithmetic Performance of Children with ADHD and Nondisabled Children," *Journal of Learning Disabilities* 29, no. 3 (1996): 238–246.

37. S. Mulligan, "Classroom Strategies Used by Teachers of Students with Attention Deficit Hyperactivity Disorder," *Physical and Occupational Therapy in Pediatrics* 20, no. 4 (2001):25–44.

alleles—Forms of a gene.

amphetamine—A group of drugs with a common chemical structure that are stimulants.

association study—An attempt to find susceptibility genes by looking at the frequency of alleles in people with ADHD and comparing it to the frequency in otherwise matched people without ADHD.

behavioral treatment—Treatment of a disorder by changing the way an individual acts rather than by using drugs.

blinded—a kind of study where the subjects do not know whether they are part of a control or treatment group. This helps to eliminate the placebo effect.

comorbid—A disorder that frequently occurs with another disorder.

concordant—Two or more the same. Concordance between monozygotic and dizygotic twin pairs is often compared as a means to estimate genetic contribution to a disorder.

conduct disorder—An *ICD-10* disorder often comorbid with hyperkinetic disorder. Conduct disorder is repeated antisocial, aggressive, or defiant behavior.

controlled study—A study conducted with two experimental groups. Both groups are treated as similarly as possible. For instance, if one group is given an injection of a drug, the other group may also be given an injection, but with no drug. The latter group is the control group.

controlled substance—A drug or other substance whose access is more tightly controlled by law, often because of the potential for addictive use, including most stimulant medications.

diagnosis—The determination of the nature of a disorder or disease.

dizygotic twins—Fraternal twins created by two separate embryos being fertilized at the same time. These twins share only 50% of their genetic material on average and are genetically the same as ordinary siblings.

dopamine—One of the main neurotransmitters in the brain with many functions, including affecting reward and attention.

double-blind trial—A type of controlled trial where one group receives drug and the other group receives placebo, but neither the patient nor the experimenter knows which group is which until the experiment is over.

DSM—The *Diagnostic and Statistical Manual of Mental Disorders*, a standard manual of many common mental disorders that is commonly used in the United States.

euphoria—A feeling of extreme pleasure and well-being, often referred to as induced by a drug.

executive function—The ability to control and execute plans and intentions.

facial tic—An involuntary occasional muscle spasm in the facial muscles. A facial tic is a common side effect of some stimulant medications.

Feingold diet—Removal of food additives and preservatives from the diet, proposed by Benjamin Feingold in the 1970s as a treatment for ADHD.

first line—The type of treatment for a disorder that is typically tried first because it has the most favorable combination of effectiveness and lack of side effects.

food allergy—An immune system response to a particular food.

gene—a unit of inheritance, often referring to the DNA sequence that codes for a particular protein.

gene therapy—Replacement or supplementation of genes—for instance, to decrease the likelihood of a disorder by causing more or less of a particular protein to be made.

genome—All of the DNA typically inherited by members of a given species.

genotype—The alleles or combinations of alleles inherited.

heritability—The extent to which a condition can be inherited from one generation to the next. Very heritable conditions commonly run in families and are more often found in relatives of an affected person than in the general population.

heterogeneous—For a genetic disorder, having many different possible genetic causes and influences.

hyperactive—More active than would usually be expected.

hyperkinetic disorder—This is the *ICD-10* equivalent of ADHD, which is somewhat different in that it requires excessive activity and inattention for the diagnosis.

hypoxia—A lack of oxygen.

ICD-10—The *International Classification of Diseases, Tenth Revision,* published by the World Health Organization.

inattentive—Having difficulty maintaining focus or attention.

introspection—The process of "looking within" to reflect on experiences.

megavitamin therapy—Treatment using large doses of vitamins, proposed for ADHD and other disorders. This treatment is dangerous if fat-soluble vitamins are included.

Mendelian disorders—Disorders mostly caused by one gene with little contribution from other genes or the environment.

monozygotic twins—Identical twins created from the splitting of one embryo. These twins share almost 100% of their genetic material.

motor breaks—Brief breaks in studying or other sedentary activity to stretch or exercise.

MRI—Magnetic resonance imaging. An MRI is often used to study changes in the brain without invasive surgery.

nanotechnology—Generation of very tiny complex structures or machines that go to where they are needed in the body to perform a task—for instance, delivering medicine.

negative reinforcement—An attempt to change a person's behavior by discouraging bad behaviors.

neural circuits—Pathways of connections between neurons.

neural correlates—Changes in the brain that occur along with changes in a phenotype.

neurons—Cells in the brain that transmit signals via neurotransmitters, forming the fundamental units of the brain.

neurotransmitters—Molecules used by neurons to transmit signals in the brain.

norepinephrine—A neurotransmitter with many functions, including effects on attention.

overdiagnosed—A condition that is diagnosed more frequently than it actually occurs, so that some people with the diagnosis do not have the condition.

overmedication—Treatment of a condition with drugs more often than is actually needed.

personalized medicine—Medical treatment that takes into account—by choice of treatment, dose, and so on—the alleles of genes in a particular person's genome.

phenocopy—An observed characteristic that is often attributed to a genetic disorder but is, in this case, being caused by an environmental factor.

phenotype—The expression of a disorder or other observable characteristic.

placebo—An ineffective treatment designed to mimic a potentially effective one—for instance, a sugar pill given in place of an actual drug.

placebo effect—An apparent change in a disorder caused by giving a placebo as a treatment. The placebo effect is caused by belief that the placebo works as a treatment, since the placebo itself is not an effective treatment.

positive reinforcement—An attempt to change a person's behavior by encouraging good behaviors.

power—In a statistical sense, the ability to detect a difference between two experimental groups.

psychiatrists—Medical doctors with specialized training in the functioning of the brain and in mental disorders.

receptors—Proteins, usually on the surface of a neuron or other cell, which respond to the amount of a neurotransmitter or other molecule that they detect.

significant—A result that has passed certain statistical criteria, often requiring that the chance of such a result occurring randomly is less than 5%.

stimulant—A type of drug that increases the activity of the nervous system.

susceptibility genes—Genes that have particular alleles that increase the likelihood of having a disorder such as ADHD.

sympathetic nervous system—The part of the nervous system responsible for speeding up and slowing down automatic responses of the body's organs, including heart rate.

symptoms—Groups of observations often found together that may be related to a disorder. For instance, a runny nose and cough may be symptoms of a cold.

synapse—The space between neurons across which neurotransmitters travel to carry signals.

transporter—A protein that removes a neurotransmitter from the synapse.

underdiagnosed—A condition that is diagnosed less frequently than it actually occurs, so that some people with the condition are not diagnosed.

undermedication—Treatment of a condition with drugs less often than is actually needed.

working memory—The type of memory responsible for temporarily storing information, such as remembering a new phone number long enough to dial it. Working memory includes processing—for instance, remembering part of the number while recalling the area code and putting it all together in order to dial the correct phone number.

FURTHER RESOURCES

Books and Articles

Adler, L., and M. Florence. *Scattered Minds: Hope and Help for Adults with ADHD.* New York: Penguin Group Inc, 2006.

Barkley, R.A. *ADHD and the Nature of Self-Control.* New York: The Guilford Press, 2005.

———. *Taking Charge of ADHD: The Complete, Authoritative Guide for Parents.* New York: The Guilford Press, 2005.

Hallowell, E.M., and J.J. Ratey. *Driven to Distraction: Recognizing and Coping with Attention Deficit Disorder from Childhood Through Adulthood.* New York: Simon & Schuster, 1995.

———. *Delivered from Distraction: Getting the Most Out of Life with Attention Deficit Disorder.* New York: Random House, 1995.

Kolberg, J., and K. Nadeau. *ADD-Friendly Ways to Organize Your Life.* New York: Taylor & Francis, Inc., 2002.

Levy, F., and D. Hay. *Attention, Genes, and ADHD.* Philadelphia: Taylor & Francis, Inc., 2003.

Nadeau, K.G., E.B. Dixon, and C. Beyl. *Learning To Slow Down & Pay Attention: A Book for Kids About ADHD.* Washington, DC: Magination Press, 2004.

Nigg, J.T. *What Causes ADHD?: Understanding What Goes Wrong and Why.* New York: The Guilford Press, 2006.

Reiff, M.I., S. Tippins, and A.A. LeTourneau. *ADHD: A Complete and Authoritative Guide.* Washington, DC: The American Academy of Pediatrics, 2004.

Wender, P.H. *Attention-Deficit Hyperactivity Disorder in Adults.* New York: Oxford University Press, 1995.

Visser, S.N., and C.A. Lesesne. "Mental Health in the United States: Prevalence of Diagnosis and Medication Treatment for Attention-Deficit/Hyperactivity Disorder: United States, 2003." *Morbidity and*

Mortality Weekly Report 54, no. 34 (September 2, 2005): 842–847. http://www.cdc.gov/mmwr/preview/mmwrhtml/mm5434a2.htm (accessed June 27, 2007).

Magazines

ADDitude
39 West 37th Street, 15th Floor
New York, NY 10018
(888) 762-8475
http://www.additudemag.com

Organizations

Children and Adults with Attention-Deficit/Hyperactivity Disorder (CHADD)
CHADD National Office
8181 Professional Place, Suite 150
Landover, MD 20785
(301) 306-7070
http://www.chadd.org

Attention Deficit Disorder Association (ADDA)
15000 Commerce Parkway, Suite C
Mount Laurel, NJ 08054
(856) 439-9099
http://www.add.org

Learning Disabilities Association of America (LDA)
4156 Library Road
Pittsburgh, PA 15234-1349
(412) 341-1515
http://www.ldaamerica.org

Web Sites

About ADD

http://add.about.com

ADD and ADHD Health Center

http://www.webmd.com/add-adhd

ADHD: A Guide for Families

http://www.aacap.org/cs/adhd_a_guide_for_families/resources_for_families_adhd_a_
   guide_for_families

ADHD.com

http://www.adhd.com

Attention-Deficit/Hyperactivity Disorder

http://www.cdc.gov/ncbddd/adhd/

Attention Deficit Hyperactivity Disorder

http://www.nimh.nih.gov/publicat/adhd.cfm

Attention Deficit Hyperactivity Disorder

http://www.nlm.nih.gov/medlineplus/attentiondeficithyperactivitydisorder.html

Focus on ADHD

http://www.focusonadhd.com

National Resource Center on AD/HD: A Program of CHADD

http://www.help4adhd.org

Understanding ADHD Information

http://www.understandingadhd.com

ABOUT THE AUTHOR

Jeremy Peirce, Ph.D., graduated from Amherst College with a B.A. in biology and earned his Ph.D. in molecular biology from Princeton University. In 2003, he went to the University of Tennessee, where he worked on microarray-derived complex trait analysis in mice. In addition to scientific writing and research, Peirce has written popular-science articles and technology/software reviews for *The Scientist, Science, Eye World Magazine*, and *Minnesota Medicine.*